Creative
Lampwork

Creative Lampwork

Techniques and Projects for the Art of Melting Glass

JOAN GORDON

Technical expert: Lesley Rands

GUILD OF MASTER
CRAFTSMAN PUBLICATION

First published 2010 by
Guild of Master Craftsman Publications Ltd
Castle Place, 166 High Street,
Lewes, East Sussex BN7 1XU

Text © Joan Gordon, 2010
© in the Work GMC Publications Ltd, 2010

ISBN 978-186108-810-9

Whilst every effort has been made to obtain permission
from the copyright holders for all the material used in the
book, the publishers will be pleased to hear from anyone
who has not been appropriately acknowledged and to
make corrections in future reprints.

The publishers and author can accept no legal
responsibility for any consequences arising from
the application of information, advice or instructions
given in this publication.

A catalog record for this book is available
from the British Library.

Associate Publisher Jonathan Bailey
Production Manager Jim Bulley
Managing Editor Gerrie Purcell
Project Editor Beth Wicks
Editor Sarah Doughty
Managing Art Editor Gilda Pacitti
Design JC Lanaway
Technical Advisor Lesley Rands

Set in Swiss and American Typewriter

Colour origination by GMC Reprographics

Printed and bound in China by C & C Offset Printing Co. Ltd

Contents

Introduction

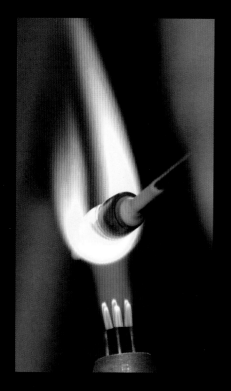

The inspiration for this book came after attending my first lampwork 'Flame Off' in Towcester, England, organized by Martin Tuffnell from Tuffnell Glass in 2008. Lampwork was not new to me but due to work commitments I'd had few chances to work 'in the flame'. This spectacular show, which is now an annual event, was the first of its kind in the UK. It gave creative-minded people the opportunity to meet with and watch professional lampwork artists in action plus the chance to try their hand at lampwork. The Flame Off was an interactive show, so those attending could experience first-hand the thrill of being able to sit at a torch and melt glass under the guidance of professional lampworkers. The organizers of the show opened a creative path for many people who until then thought that lampwork was an expensive, highly skilled craft, well beyond the average person's ability.

Whilst lampwork was once the proudly protected craft of the Venetians, it has become one of the fastest developing crafts throughout the world. As a well-established hobby and creative art form in America since the early 1900s, it came into its own in the UK when the West Midlands-based glass manufacturers Plowden and Thompson offered lampwork bead classes in 1997. Since then, as in most other countries that have embraced this craft, lampwork associations have been formed in the UK to support glass artists, to assist in selling their work and offer the opportunity to network with fellow artists, nationally and internationally. Today, glass beadmaking and lampwork glass sculpting continue to draw more and more creative souls to the flame.

Working as an editor for jewellery and bead magazines has given me the privilege of working with many highly talented lampwork artists. As my interest in lampwork increased, it was inspirational to bring together the skills of these talented lampworkers to assist in creating a practical and instructional introduction for the novice lampwork enthusiast. This has turned into this book, an aspirational resource for those who have already invested in the craft as a serious hobby or career path.

With the help of Lesley Rands, the talented lampwork artist who has contributed most of the technical step-by-step instructions and photographs for making beads, this book brings together both technical expertise and practical ideas. You will see the extensive and clearly illustrated techniques for both making and decorating glass beads. Together with lampworking artists showing how to make their own projects, there are many beautiful and creative ideas here that should inspire others to explore the magical world of glass.

JOAN GORDON

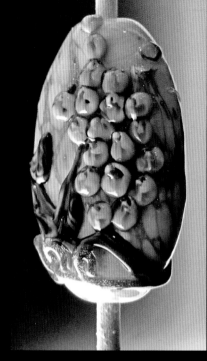

The History of Lampwork

In 1291 Italian glassmakers from the Venetian Republic moved their foundries to Murano, which is situated 1 mile (1.5 km) north of Venice in the Venetian Lagoon. It was this move that made the community in Murano famous for its glassmaking, which was the result of the widespread fear of fire breaking out amongst its wooden houses. Murano consists of a series of little islands linked by bridges, and is still home to 7,000 people today.

Murano is popular with visitors who come to explore its many factories and artists' studios.

The History of Glass

Glassmaking in Murano is thought to have originated from trade with Rome in the 9th century and to have Asian and Muslim influences. By the fourteenth century the glassmakers of Murano were the island's most prominent citizens. They intermarried with the most wealthy and respected Venetian families and were immune from prosecution by the Venetian State. Despite their special privileges and social status, the law prevented the glassmakers from leaving the republic in an attempt to protect their craft. If caught trying to leave, the penalty was death. These craftsmen held the key to several highly complex glass making techniques including crystalline glass, enamelled glass (smalto), glass with threads of gold (aventurine), multicoloured glass, milk glass (lattimo), and imitation gemstones made of glass. Their skills remained a well-guarded secret from the rest of the world, which made Venice such a rich port for traders.

It was only due to the risks taken by craftsmen who wished to travel and experience life abroad that glass making and furnaces sprang up in surrounding cities and abroad.

Lampwork has become famous in Murano. However, the actual origins of lampwork beads are not certain.

There is evidence that glass was being used to make beads in Ancient Egypt, Mesopotamia and parts of Asia dating back to the first century AD. In the fourteenth century lampworking came into its own in Italy where Italian artists melted glass in a flame to create their own unique beads. The technique or making lampwork beads has changed very little over the centuries; lampworking is possible thanks to the technology that is available today. The various torches and tools that are on sale today make lampwork an increasingly accessible artistic craft for both amateur and professional lampworkers alike.

For hundreds of years Murano has been considered the home of lampwork and Venetian glass. Whilst most of the inhabitants were involved in the glass industry in the seventeenth century, today the number of factories and private studios in Murano is considerably fewer.

A Centre for Glass Enthusiasts

For tourists, glass artists and lampwork enthusiasts, Murano is still considered a romantic destination and the world leader for glass collectables, exquisite beads and unique jewellery. For the aspiring glass artist to attend lampwork or glassblowing workshops run by a master craftsman in a studio on Murano is a dream many people hope one day to realize.

If you are passionate about the art of lampwork, glass blowing or glass sculpture and are fortunate enough to find yourself on the shores of this labyrinth of lanes, traditional homes,

palaces, shops and bridges, a visit to the glass Museum Museo del Vetro-Fondamenta Guistiniani 8 is a must. The museum is within Palazzo Giustiniani, which is situated on the Grand Canal, and it houses various collections of glass works depicting the history of glassmaking. The museum has samples of glass from Egyptian times through to the present day, and the displays show glass developed over the centuries. A visit will expand and broaden your knowledge of and love for all things glass.

Contemporary glass vases on display in Murano.

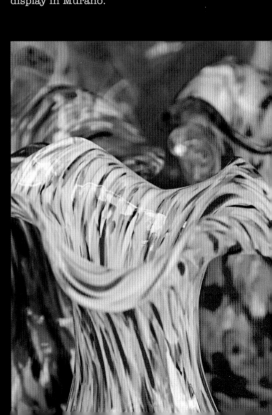

Shaping molten glass has been part of Murano's history for centuries.

This ornament shaped using a flame is typical of Murano glassmaking

One of the many stands of glass beads on sale for tourists in Venice.

In fact, it has never been easier to set up as a lampwork artist, and only a small amount of equipment is needed to get going. A simple lampwork station can be set up in the home or in a garden shed, provided strict safety rules are followed.

pricing, which in turn has opened up business opportunities that once would not have been available to the average person. Ebay and Etsy have made it possible for people to have their own online shops where they can showcase their work and sell to collectors or fellow artists who use lampwork beads to make jewellery, gifts and homewares.

The internet has allowed artists to communicate globally via forums and live chat rooms. Video streaming gives anyone interested in lampwork the opportunity to watch tutorials online, make friends and share their passion with like-minded people. Lampwork communities exist in almost every country and through such forums. No matter how isolated you may be geographically, you are never alone if you have access to the internet.

Beautiful lampwork bead jewellery is popular all over the world.

that are free to join.

Lampwork groups and associations have been formed in several countries. These societies are welcoming to new members and are helpful for anyone interested in learning more about this craft. Most of these groups aim to support their members through exhibitions, bead fairs and in raising their members' profiles.

As more experienced artists are now teaching lampwork, it is possible to join a class or course nearly anywhere in the world. Studios with multiple torches have been developed in several countries where tutors specializing in specific techniques offer short- and long-term lampwork classes. This interchange of skills and the opportunity to travel and study abroad opens new doors to the exchange of ideas and creative experimentation.

Another View

Benjamin Evers, a lampworking artist based in British Columbia, Canada, sums up well the global view of lampwork today. He says, 'The last few years seem to me to have brought about major changes to the artistic lampworking movement. New tools, colours, techniques and technology; the sharing of information over the internet; and the integration of other forms of arts and crafts and their media. All these are now blending and the results are spectacular. Advancements for the borosilicate lampworker specifically have been dramatic. The addition of new colour manufacturers has aided the growth of both objects and ideas. No longer is the artistic lampworker restricted by scale, palette, or even medium; only by imagination, skill and, of course, the insatiable need for better tools and more space. Hardly a day goes by that there isn't something new and amazing produced somewhere within our community... It is a great time indeed for lampworking. Thanks to networking websites we now are able to connect with our peers, drawing inspiration from one another while forming new links, organizations, bonds and great friendships with each other. I think this is a major contribution to the fire that keeps us advancing together on a daily level.

What's in store for the future I wonder? I can only imagine that objects of increasing beauty will be being made by people just like you and me... and that glass will still be as captivating as ever... I would say lampworking is definitely in the midst of a revival, perhaps even a revolution. Viva la revolución!'

There is endless creativity in the art of lampwork due to the current revival.

Gallery

Here are some of the amazing beads and glass designs that have been contributed by the team of talented lampwork artists in the Projects section. Lampwork beads are not used exclusively for jewellery making; some of the beautiful beads are used to decorate items for the home and for personal gifts.

Cone Pendant
Dawn Lombard
Shaped at an angle to form a cone, this pendant is also beautifully decorated (pages 140–141).

Graceful Eastern Bead
Anita Schwegler-Juen
Intricate layers of dots decorate this piece to make a versatile pendant (pages 158–159).

Organic Paperknife
Jan Jennings
A knife handle created with golden tones and fine detail (pages 130–131).

Encased Bead Bracelet
Beverley Hicklin
Made up of layers
of transparent colour,
with lengths of twisted
glass for decoration
(pages 118–121).

Grapevine Pendant
Jan Jennings
A raised grapevine
design on a focal
bead, made into
a necklace
(pages 128–129).

Victoriana Bead
and Victoriana Silver Core
Amanda Muddimer
Beads made with silver glass,
lined with silver at their core
(pages 146–149).

Grecian Vessel Pendant
Elaine Aldeheff
Made with cobalt blue glass
and delicately decorated
(pages 108–111).

Bead Ring
Emma Baird
This sets a beautiful
blue lampwork
bead securely on
top of a silver ring
(pages 114–115).

Bead Earrings
Emma Baird
Made from lentil-
shaped beads and
decorated with silver
leaf and mesh
(pages 112–113).

Squiggle Bead Necklace
Pauline Holt
Celebrates colour in
the form of a necklace
(pages 124–125).

Champagne Bead Stopper
Beverley Hicklin
A beautiful marbling effect
is created in the glass bead
(pages 122–123).

Butterfly Pate Knife
Sabine Little
Uses relief sculpture
of a flower and butterfly
design on a bicone bead
(pages 132–133).

Floral Beaded Pen
Sabine Little
Made with round beads decorated with delicate flowers (pages 136–137).

Beads for Rings
Dawn Lombard
A ring with replaceable beads ready to suit any occasion (pages 142–143).

Ruffle Bead Spoon
Sabine Little
Created using blue glass decorated with gold leaf (pages 134–135).

Peacock Bead Bracelet
Lorna Prime
Delicate features in turquoise and purple are combined with unique findings (pages 150–151).

Swirl Bead Pendant
Amanda Muddimer
Makes clever use of
gravity and Triton glass
(pages 144–145).

Celestial Bead
Bookmark
Lorna Prime
Designed around the
bookmark hook and
features a beautiful
blue focal bead
(pages 152–153).

Ivy Leaf Pendant
Sandra Young
Uses fine leaf
detailing and
made with
borosilicate glass
(pages 164–167).

Sea Anemone Pendant
Marcel Rensmagg
The technique traps
bubbles to create a
sea anemone effect
in these pendants
(pages 154–157).

Funky Fish Earrings
Sue Webb
Sculptured beads
created with a touch
of fish frivolity
(pages 160–161).

Twisted Light Pull
Sandra Young
Uses tapered as well as
twisted borosilicate glass
(pages 162–163).

Urn Bead
Dawn Lombard
Created from a cone-
shaped bead and
simply decorated
(pages 138–139).

Catwalk Necklace
Pauline Holt
Made from borosilicate
and dichroic glass to form
a large sculptural necklace
(pages 126–127).

How to use this Book

This book has been designed to guide a complete novice in how to make a lampwork bead and is a valuable resource for the more skilled lampworker who wants to explore alternative ideas and techniques.

Working Safely

The issues that are covered first are aspects of safely working at a torch. It cannot be emphasized enough the importance of safety in creating a space to set up your lampwork tools and torch or when working with an open flame that is fuelled with gas or a gas and oxygen mix. Pages 26 –29 cover the safety aspects in some detail. It is important for anyone considering lampwork as a serious hobby to be well aware of safety issues before experimenting.

Knowing the Basics

To create a finished piece that you can be proud of, it helps to be familiar with the best lampwork tools for the job. A comprehensive section focusing on what materials and equipment to use when making lampwork beads can be found on pages 30–41.

Learning the Techniques

Professional lampwork artist, Lesley Rands, expertly demonstrates how to manipulate and use these tools in the Melting Glass and Decorative Techniques pages (42–65 and 66–105). There are many different ways to complete each technique, here we have concentrated on just the one. The professional artists in the creative Projects section also use some of these techniques. Their exciting bead designs on pages 106–167 really show lampwork in action. The possibilities of what can be made using glass as a medium and the decorative techniques that may be employed to make one of these bespoke artefacts are infinite.

With a little experience you will soon master the techniques of lampworking. However, you must be determined to practise, practise, then practise some more, to achieve good results. It is also important to respect the flame you are working with whilst not being afraid of it. If you are new to lampwork, a few lessons with an experienced teacher will help you overcome the initial fear of molten glass and open your mind and soul to a passion that will stay with you for life.

In Melting Glass, try making different shapes of bead.

In Decorative Techniques, try different methods of decorating a bead.

In Projects, make special items for the home and jewellery to wear.

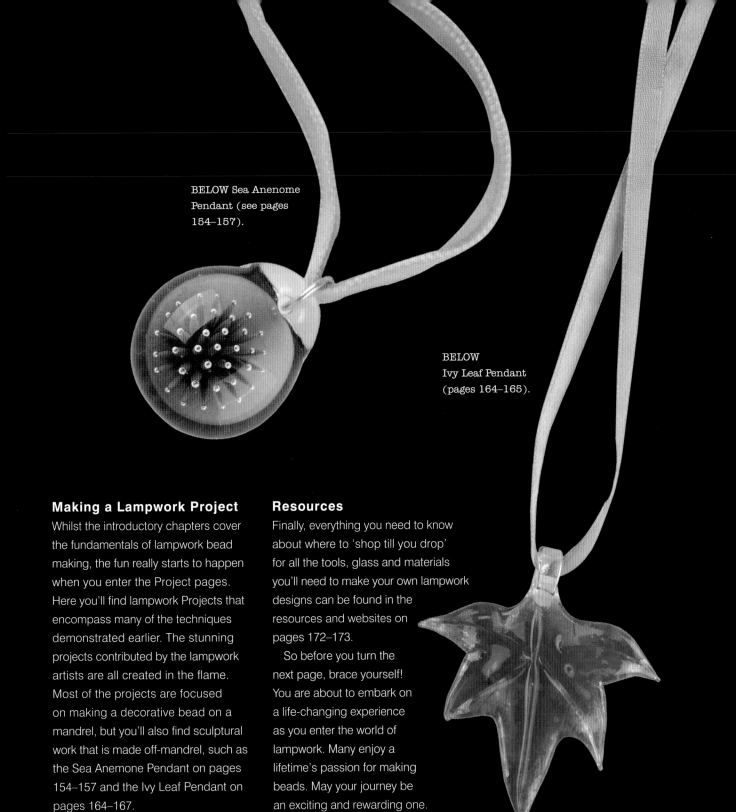

BELOW Sea Anenome Pendant (see pages 154–157).

BELOW Ivy Leaf Pendant (pages 164–165).

Making a Lampwork Project

Whilst the introductory chapters cover the fundamentals of lampwork bead making, the fun really starts to happen when you enter the Project pages. Here you'll find lampwork Projects that encompass many of the techniques demonstrated earlier. The stunning projects contributed by the lampwork artists are all created in the flame. Most of the projects are focused on making a decorative bead on a mandrel, but you'll also find sculptural work that is made off-mandrel, such as the Sea Anemone Pendant on pages 154–157 and the Ivy Leaf Pendant on pages 164–167.

Resources

Finally, everything you need to know about where to 'shop till you drop' for all the tools, glass and materials you'll need to make your own lampwork designs can be found in the resources and websites on pages 172–173.

So before you turn the next page, brace yourself! You are about to embark on a life-changing experience as you enter the world of lampwork. Many enjoy a lifetime's passion for making beads. May your journey be an exciting and rewarding one.

LAMPWORK BASICS
Learning about tools and safe practice

This section will show you the basic tools that you will need to set up in lampworking and how to create a safe workshop. Apart from a torch, gas supply and a kiln, most of the tools are relatively inexpensive. If you're not sure whether you are serious about lampwork as a creative hobby or an artistic venture, then it's possible to start with simply a Hot Head torch and a basic tool kit (see page 31). Many suppliers offer beginner kits which make the initial entry into lampwork possible. When setting up a lampwork station, stocking up on a few of these basic tools will be sufficient to get you going until you are ready to experiment further. There are many more exciting tools to purchase, but keep it simple for now while you get used to the basics.

CREATING A SAFE WORKPLACE

Before setting up a lampwork station it is important to understand fundamental safety procedures. Unsafe handling of gas and other volatile materials can cause injury or even death. Contact a recognized lampwork association and/or professional lampwork tutor and ask for advice before setting up a workshop at home.

Check your own local regulations to ensure that your workshop is a safe working environment for undertaking creative lampwork.

Torches

All torches used for lampwork (see pages 32–33) are tools that produce a very hot flame. Care must be taken at all times when lighting and working with a lampwork torch. From the very basic Hot Head to the mid-range Nortel Minors, Bethlehem SGA hand-held and the high-end National (which has a multi-hole tip), they all require fuel to fire them. Before purchasing a torch, discuss this with several lampwork artists and manufacturers. Check out what's on offer to be sure that you purchase a torch that will suit your needs. Take the time to understand how it is used, what fuel it requires and how to maintain it safely.

Getting Started

When setting up a workshop ensure that you have good ventilation, such as an extractor fan. You will need a fireproof workstation with overhead-lighting power switches and leads installed by a qualified electrician. All propane gas bottles need to be fitted with a regulator and should have flashback arrestors. These should always be supplied and maintained by a registered gas company. The cylinders should be securely positioned according to the regulations specific to your local area. Always ask a qualified gasfitter to fit your unit in order to ensure your own safety.

Working with Gas

Natural gas or other similar fuel may be used alone or in combination with oxygen for a variety of torches on the market. Propane is a liquefied petroleum gas that is often used in lampwork. If you have access to natural gas then a regulator is not required. Propane gas can also be used and mixed with oxygen to fuel dual-feed torches.

It is not advisable to have propane gas bottles in the home. They can be safely stored outside a studio or home workshop and fitted with a regulator and flashback arrestors incorporating a one-way gas flow valve and sintered flame trap to increase the safety of the oxy-acetylene process. Check to see what laws are in place in your county, state or country of residence. Don't get caught out, as these regulations can incur a fine if you are found to be working in an unsafe workshop and it is dangerous for you.

Propane is extracted from both natural and refinery gases. It is normally a vapour gas at temperatures above its boiling point at -44 °F (-42.2°C). The boiling point is the temperature at which the liquid gas will convert into vapour at atmospheric pressure. When it is compressed into a liquid state it will remain a liquid under pressure when stored in special pressure containers, such as a cylinder. When converting to vapour-liquid, propane expands to about 270 times its liquid volume. This is why so much heating value (British Thermal Units, or BTUs) can be stored in small containers. It also explains why escaping liquid gas causes more problems than an identical-sized vapour leak.

Propane is odorized to give it an uncommon odour that smells like rotten eggs. Store your gas bottle upright. Should you smell this gas or even suspect a leak, turn the lampwork torch and the valve at the container off.

This gas isn't called a silent killer for no reason. Do not check for a leak by igniting a match. Escaping gas will seek out low places and collect creating a flammable mixture that can explode. Check your connections and hoses regularly. Connections can be checked for possible leaks with soapy water or propane leak detection solution – if bubbles form on a connection, you know that there is a leak in it. If you think you may have a problem, turn off the propane at the source and contact your local propane dealer for advice.

Hoses

These come in different grades. The safest to use when lampworking is Grade T. This is a heavy rubber hose which is flame resistant. Ask your supplier to provide you with the correct hoses for your set-up, each of which should be firmly connected to your gas and oxygen supplies.

Learn from experienced lampworkers how to work a flame safely. It can help to go to events to pick up tips and talk to the experts.

Propane bottle attached to a simple regulator and flash arrestor. The regulator controls the pressure of gas from the cylinder to the torch.

The Nortel Minor burner requires a supply of propane (via the top tube) and a supply of oxygen (via the bottom tube) to function correctly.

Ventilation

Good ventilation is vital to ensure a safe workshop, and an extractor fan should be installed near each torch station. The lampworking torch produces hazardous fumes from the high-temperature flame reacting with the nitrogen in the air. Over time breathing in these fumes will damage your lungs. Ensure your workspace is well ventilated at all times. Using an open window to get rid of fumes is not enough as many of the coloured glasses used in lampwork contain chemicals that vaporize and can lead to serious health problems.

Oxygen

You can lease oxygen tanks and regulators from your local supply company. Alternatively, an Oxy-con unit is a machine that makes oxygen. Oxy-con is short for 'oxygen converter concentrator'. It is a machine that takes in air and separates out the oxygen, so you can use a torch that needs two fuels (gas and oxygen) without an oxygen tank. If you are using a torch that needs a mix of gas and oxygen, then it's a cost-effective and safe way of producing the oxygen part of the mix. Depending on the type of torch and glass that you are working with, you will be able to determine the size and type of machine that will work best for you.

An Oxy-con is usually a reconditioned medical unit available from suppliers.

With portable freestanding oxygen bottles, the cost of renting one of these varies depending on location. They are usually hired from the supplier and you pay a security deposit on the bottle. The large tanks are more economical to fill, but heavier to carry than the smaller ones. If workspace is limited, a small bottle or an oxy-con will serve the purpose. The oxygen bottle must be secured safely in your workshop to prevent it from being knocked over. Once the tank is empty, it is taken back and traded for a full one. There are two basic types of oxygen regulators – single and two-stage. Two-stage regulators are the most common because they deliver a more constant pressure. They are more expensive than a single stage but then again,

more effective. Do some research online and also ask professional lampworkers what they recommend before you invest in any lampworking tools and supplies.

Glasses

When working at a torch it is important that safety glasses are worn at all times to project your eyes. Sunglasses, clear safety glasses and reading glasses do not offer protection from the yellow sodium flare (589NM), which occurs when working and melting glass in a torch flame.

Didymium glass is a special glass that absorbs the bright yellow sodium flare and allows safe viewing of a bead as it is worked in the flame. This glass is used in freestanding protective glass frames, face shields, clip-on glasses and in a variety of spectacle frames. For the novice lampworker, using MAPP gas or propane torches with soft, soda-lime glass offers some protection. They should also be used when viewing beads in the kiln or when checking on fused glass in the kiln. Didymium glasses are made from polycarbonate. Even though they may look unattractive, the glasses with side

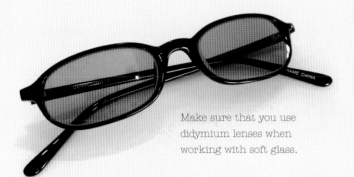

Make sure that you use didymium lenses when working with soft glass.

Safety

The safety information here only touches on this important subject. For comprehensive advice contact your local Health and Safety Authority. See also the safety checklist on page 41.

frames offer more projection than clip-on frames that can be used over prescription glasses or the more modern styles that look like sunglasses. Didymium glasses and shields are not recommended for high-pressure torch flames that are used for melting hard glass, Pyrex or quartz, and they definitely shouldn't be worn for furnace glassblowing.

The high temperature glass rods, sheet and shards such as borosilicate require more sophisticated eye protection. Aura Lens Products make AUR-186, which will filter infrared and damaging wavelengths. With new advances in technology, smaller and lighter lenses have been created that are more comfortable to wear and less expensive than the original protective glasses. Lampwork glasses not only protect your eyes from the potentially damaging wavelengths but also from flying shards of glass that, if they were to hit your eye, may otherwise cause permanent damage.

Kilns

When using a kiln to anneal your glass beads you must wear protective heatproof gloves and safety glasses. Kilns are a major investment, so read the manufacturer's instructions to maintain safety and to develop a clear understanding of their functions.

Other Precautions

Keep a fire extinguisher and blanket on hand for small fires, as well as cool water and burn spray for accidents.

A bench-mount didymium shield mask is another type of face and eye protection to use in a workshop.

Keep a fire extinguisher and a fire blanket in good working order and easily accessible.

A spray for superficial burns and blistering is useful to have to hand in a workshop.

MARVERS AND TOOLS

A marver is a flat or semi-flat working surface that can be made from graphite or brass. Marvers come in various shapes and sizes, with or without handles, and are used in both lampwork and glassblowing. Here are some of the marvers used in lampwork and some of the tools used to shape glass.

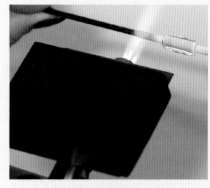

A BoroTube torch-mounted marver acts as a shelf to keep glass warm.

A paddle marver is made from graphite and is multipurpose.

Marvering paddles are simply a marver with a handle attached. They can be made from graphite (or brass can also be used). Paddles are used to roll glass on, to assist in creating a shape, to smooth or apply foils, frit, enamel or other decorations to molten glass.

Torch-mounted Marvers

Several different-sized detachable marvers are available from lampwork suppliers. These marvers are designed so that they attach to the torch. This will make using the marver easy to access. Having one attached to a torch frees up your second hand and also helps having to search for a paddle when working in the flame.

Marble-domed Marvers

These graphite pads have marble domes cut into the graphite on one side and are flat on the other. The flat side is similar to all flat graphite marvers and can be used to flatten beads or place frit and millifiore on before use. The domed side is used to hold frits and enamels or to shape glass.

A domed marver containing enamel powder, where a hot bead can be rolled in the powder.

Graphite Marvers

A graphite marver is used to shape the beads and to assist in several decorative techniques. The importance of graphite in lampwork is due to its very low density and its ability to absorb heat. Graphite marvers are used to touch the molten glass and, as there is minimal temperature contrast between the metal and glass, it absorbs the heat energy. There is minimal shock to the glass and this is exactly what is required when creating beads or simply working with molten glass.

Brass presses come in an assortment of sizes and shapes for pressing and shaping hot beads.

Basic tools for your worktop:

Here are some tools that you will find useful for lampworking.

1. Leaf pliers
For pressing and shaping glass.

2. Glass scissors
For cutting hot glass.

3. Pointed tweezers
For all fine work.

4. Paddle marver
Surface for marvering.

5. Mashers
For pressing and shaping glass.

6. Shaping tool
For flutes, spirals and twists.

7. Single-sided razor tool
To create patterns and shape beads.

8. Pick
To poke, rake and drag.

9. Straight-edged tool
For cuts and indentations.

10. Tungsten rake
Another tool to poke, rake and drag.

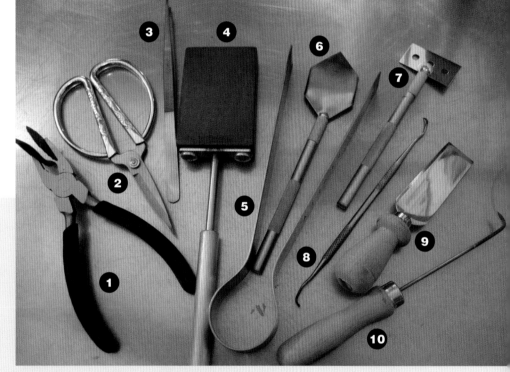

Brass Tools and Moulds

Tools made of brass are also ideal for marvering, shaping and moulding glass. Brass has a little more 'tooth' to it than graphite, and as such, can 'push' the glass around better than graphite. Brass takes longer than graphite to get hot. Brass tools such as marvers, moulds and shaping tools are used in lampwork when you want to cool something off quickly. The raku-coloured glasses such as the Reichenbach range respond well to rapid heating and cooling cycles. When the glass is cooled quickly after heating it to a molten state, it helps the raku colours to bloom.

Brass moulds and presses come in a variety of different designs and are ideal for creating uniformly shaped beads. The designs of brass presses vary slightly, but they all come with a base and a top. The base may have brass dowels protruding upwards and indentations for both the mandrel and the glass bead. The top has the same indentations but two holes for the base dowels to align into. Brass is a cold metal and will shock the glass when it comes into contact with it, if you are not careful. Preheat the press by placing it on top of the kiln before placing any hot glass inside.

LAMPWORK TORCHES

There are a number of different types of torches available for making lampwork beads and melting glass. The least expensive and most frequently bought by novice lampwork enthusiasts is the Hot Head torch. However, make sure it suits your needs before you buy one as there are many other brands and types of torches available.

Fuel Only

There are many lampwork artists who use only the Hot Head torch and need nothing else. Several companies offer starter kits that include this torch, and this is a good way of getting into lampworking. This torch only uses gas as fuel and doesn't require oxygen.

This is because it has large air intake holes below the head that allow it to take in air to maximize the temperature of the flame. It can be worked with cylinders of MAPP gas or propane. These cylinders can be purchased in hardware stores or speciality gas suppliers and are readily available in most countries. However, because the flame is not separately oxygenated, the fuel gas can sometimes steal oxygen from the glass. This can result in the darkening of light-coloured glass, which may not make this torch ideal for all lampworking jobs. It is, however, ideal for the beginner.

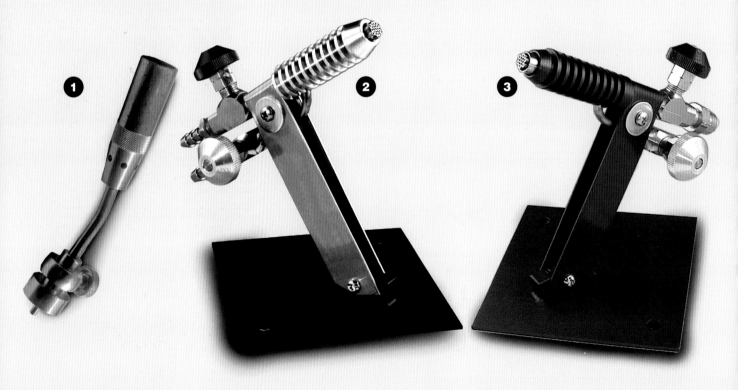

Dual-fuel Mix

Torches that require a mix of oxygen and fuel are more expensive but vary considerably in price. The Minor Burner made by Nortel is perfect for working with soft glass and more recently the new Mega Minor allows for working on harder borosilicate glass. The combustion of the propane is more complete and a higher flame temperature is reached than by just MAPP gas or propane on its own. It is used for making beads and for small sculptural work.

Dual-fuel torches require a gas supply such as propane from a tank, and an oxygen supply from either a tank or an oxygen concentrator. You can buy or rent an oxygen tank that can be refilled or you can use an Oxy-con unit. If you decide to work with hard glass you will possibly need two concentrators hooked up together or an oxygen tank, as borosilicate glass requires a hotter flame.

Other Torches

There are many brands and types of lampwork torches available, including the Lynx burner, Isiheat, Piranha, Wale Firebird, Carlisle Mini CC (and Carlisle Bench Burner) and the Bobcat. This is not a comprehensive list of what is available and all torches have various advantages and disadvantages. To learn more about torches, surf the internet and make enquiries through your favourite lampwork association.

The best way to find a torch that suits your needs is to try different torches out by doing some workshops with professional teachers. It's up to you to find a torch that fires your imagination and lets you produce your best work. Remember that you can start with a relatively inexpensive torch to discover whether lampworking is for you, and upgrade to a different torch later.

BELOW LEFT TO RIGHT
1. Hot Head torch.
2. Nortel Minor torch.
3. Nortel Minor torch.
4. Carlisle Mini CC torch.
5. Carlisle Wildcat torch.

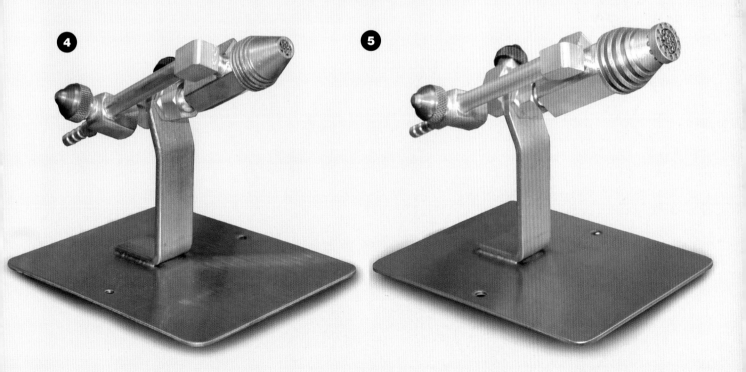

GLASS FOR LAMPWORKING

There are several types of glass used by lampwork artists and here we introduce a few of the ones most frequently used and their characteristics.

Effetre Glass

This is one of the most famous brand names for glass. Effetre was originally developed for industrial purposes and is now used by lampworkers. It is Italian glass that was first produced over 500 years ago in Venice by the Ferro family, who founded the glass factory. There is still a factory in Murano today, but the headquarters of the Effetre company is in Resana where the manufacturer produces blown, pressed and centrifugal glass components for thousands of different companies around the world.

Soda-lime Glass

One of the most common types of glass used for lampwork is soda-lime. This is a called a soft glass because it melts at fairly low temperatures. Traditionally it was a mix used in blown furnace glass and rods were hand-drawn from the furnace. Today it is manufactured globally, sold in rods of various thicknesses and produced in a wide array of colours. It is important when using soda-glass that the colours chemically and in terms of compatible COE (coefficient of thermal expansion). If incompatible glasses are mixed

together, this can create stresses within a finished piece as it cools. This will cause cracking or the piece may even shatter. Soda-glass and borosilicate glass are not compatible with each other and should be labelled and stored separately.

Borosilicate Glass

Hard borosilicate glass is frequently used in lampwork. It is a tough glass because it requires higher temperatures to bring it to melting point than soda-glass. Borosilicate is a laboratory glass and has a lower COE than soda-glass, which makes it more forgiving to work with and less inclined to crack during lampwork. This glass is more expensive than soda-lime glass but is often the favoured medium by lampwork artists who enjoy sculpting with glass. Borosilicate has a higher working range than soda-lime glass and therefore requires larger torches which are fuelled by a mix of oxygen and gas. In producing a hotter flame the use of pure oxygen allows more control over the oxidizing or reducing properties in the glass. Some borosilicate glass, which has been chemically coloured, will react with the oxygen in the flame, which can affect the final colour of the glass sculpture or bead that has been made. Hence the importance of being able to correctly control the mix of oxygen, gas and heat of the flame.

Lead Glass

Lampworkers sometimes use lead glass in lampwork and lead glass is noted for its lower viscosity, heavier weight and greater tolerance for COE mismatches. The high lead content makes it sparkle more than other types of glass, but also makes it more fragile. The popularity of lead glass has reduced in recent years as the range and availability of different types of glass has increased.

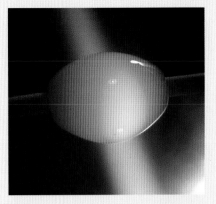

Coloured soft glass is used for most lampwork bead projects.

Borosilicate glass requires a larger flame but is less inclined to crack during working than soft glass. It is often used for sculpting projects, such as creating this ivy leaf.

Speciality Glass Rods

Metalized special glass rods called reduction glass are also available. Double Helix is one such glass that has become very popular for making decorative glass beads. These glasses need attention to the final heat process that causes the metal oxides (gold and silver) to settle on the surface. To achieve this the oxygen content is reduced in the torch flame and the bead covered in the reduction glass is wafted gently in the fuel-rich flame, until the metalized effect is achieved.

Striking glass is similar to reduction glass in that it develops its true colour only when it has been melted, cooled and gently reheated. The striking rods are pale transparent in colour and they only reach their full attractive colours when the working is complete.

Stringers are used for decoration and can be commercially bought or made.

Striking glass rods and beads in yellow, orange and ruby gold.

Rods, Sheets, Stringers and Frits

Most lampworkers favour working with glass rods. The most popular sizes of rod used for lampwork range from ¼–⅝in (6–15mm) in diameter. With experience, thin rods of glass, called stringers, can be pulled in the flame of a torch from these glass rods. Many lampwork artists create their own plain, twisted and multicoloured stringers to use to decorate their beads. Pre-made stringers are available most commonly in sizes of ⅟₃₂–⅛in (1–3mm), but many

Frits can be home-made or commercially bought. Bought frit is available in varying sizes from fine through to large.

Dichroic glass has a coated and uncoated side and is available in different forms, including the sheet and frit.

sizes of stringer are available. Sheet glass, which is mainly used for fusing, can be cut with tools into strips, though it is easier to manipulate if attached to a rod first. The rod of glass is used as a punty. The tip of the rod and end of the sheet glass are both heated in the flame and then pressed together. Once melded the sheet can be more easily manipulated in the flame with the dominant hand controlling it via the attached rod. Glass is also available in particles of various sizes (frit or powder), which is used for surface decoration. Many manufacturers who once only sold their glass in sheet or very thick rod now provide rods for lampworking use.

Wine, mineral water and soft drink bottles can also be broken into shards and used like sheet glass to make glass beads. It is important to check the COE of the glass if you plan to mix it with alternative glass rods, stringers or frits, as they may not be compatible.

Dichroic glass

The word 'dichroic' means two colours. It is thought that dichroic glass was first made in the late 1800s in Germany by Dr Arthur Pfeiffer. In the 1960s NASA developed a highly technical method of producing it to make windows for space vessels. Once this method was fine tuned, the glass was manufactured on a large scale which led to it becoming sufficiently inexpensive enough that it could be used in glassblowing, fusing and lampwork.

Dichroic glass is made from very thin layers of glass with several rare metals placed on the surface of a piece of glass. The glass is placed in a vacuum chamber and bombarded with an intense electron beam. This beam vaporizes some of the material, which in turn coats vibrant colours onto the sheet of glass.

If you view this glass from different angles you will see a variety of colours as you rotate it. When the glass is held in the hand one colour is seen by reflected light, tilt the glass and another

Dichroic glass is attached in the flame.

colour will shine through it. If you view dichroic glass to the side it is completely clear. Wavelengths of light transmit and reflect through the glass creating different iridescent surface colours.

KILNS

A kiln is an insulated chamber that heats up to between 1,697–2,363°F (925–1,295°C). At these temperatures, materials change and burn away, fuse, harden or melt. You can control a kiln's heating, holding and cooling, and the time it takes. Most kilns have some sort of controller. At the very least this is a rotary heating control, and at best a comprehensive digital programmer.

Small Kilns

The Paragon SC-2 (SC meaning Silver Clay) is one of most popular small kilns. It is inexpensive, easy to use and programmable; ideal for making jewellery. Certain materials such as glass, ceramic and precious metal clays can be annealed and fired or melted in a kiln. You can set it to run a long sequence of heating, holding and cooling automatically. You can be sure that the heating and cooling rate is optimized, that your work reaches or stays at the right temperature for the right time and that the whole piece heats uniformly. Other kilns, such as the Paragon Bluebird are similar and are also widely used.

Firing Chamber

The firing chamber is usually made of ceramic fibre or firebricks and held together by a steel case. The heating elements are usually coils of wire, which for safety are embedded in the fibre and are turned off if the kiln door is opened. Depending on the design,

The Paragon SC-2 is a popular choice of kiln; there are some variations between kilns in the SC series.

Paragon SC-2

- Temperature 2,000°F (1,095°C)
- Door opens 180° for easy loading
- Interior chamber size @ 8 x 8 x 5in (20 x 20 x 13cm)
- Outer size @ 13 x 14 x 15in (33 x 36 x 38cm)
- Elements in ceramic fibre (heats from top and/or sides)
- Sentry Xpress 3-key digital programmer

Paragon BlueBird

- Temperature 1,200°F (650°C)
- Outward opening, twin doors
- Interior chamber size @ 20 x 5 x 5in (50 x 12 x 12cm)
- Outer size @ 33 x 11 x 13in (85 x 29 x 34cm)
- Elements in ceramic fibre (heats from top)
- Sentry Xpress 3-key digital programmer

the firing chamber heats from opposite sides, the top, or a mix of sides, top, front and back. To protect the floor of the firing chamber, work usually stands on a shelf, fibre cloth or ceramic block.

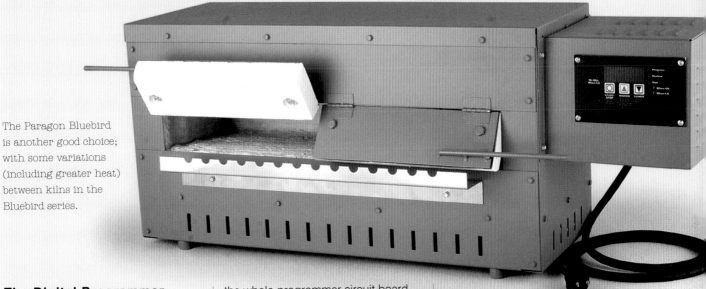

The Paragon Bluebird is another good choice; with some variations (including greater heat) between kilns in the Bluebird series.

The Digital Programmer

The thermocouple usually projects into the firing chamber at the back. It is basically a join between two dissimilar metals that, when heated, generates a tiny voltage that can be converted by the digital programmer to a temperature. The digital programmer has a display, which shows the set temperature and times and can be set by using keys. The programmer compares its programming instructions to the thermocouple's current temperature and the time the kiln has been on. It then decides whether to turn the elements on or off.

The Relay and Transformer

A relay is an electronic switch. The programmer uses a low voltage to activate the relay, which then turns the high voltage elements on. The relay keeps the high voltage away from the programmer and, should it fail, it's much cheaper to replace the relay than the whole programmer circuit board. During firing you can hear the relay clicking on and off. The transformer turns the mains voltage into 12V for the programmer. A low-voltage unit is cheaper to make and safer to use.

How Kilns Work

All programmable kilns work in the same way: the thermocouple checks the internal temperature regularly and tells the programmer to switch the elements on or off in order to control the heating, holding or cooling.

When the target temperature is reached, the elements are switched off. However, residual heat in the firing chamber allows the internal temperature to overshoot its target briefly before starting to fall back. Take this into account if you're working with temperature-critical materials or processes. During the hold-time, the internal temperature falls. Although the programmer will soon switch the elements back on, the firing chamber will initially absorb some of the new heat before the temperature recovers. The continual switching of the elements on and off causes variations in the internal temperature. Your work will be affected slightly by its position on the kiln shelf, the vertical spacing of any stacked shelves, a lid, a door, a bead door, window or peephole.

Glass needs radiant heat and is better on one shelf than between stacked shelves. Kiln doors and lids are not meant to be a perfect fit, otherwise there would be no room for expansion and the door could stick and the firebricks could crack. With normal use, kilns discolour slightly inside and outside, and some firebricks might develop hairline cracks. Remember, your kiln is a robust, versatile, red-hot tool, not an ornament.

PREPARING FOR LAMPWORK

Before you start lampwork you will need to set up your torch and tools and prepare the mandrels ready to create a lampwork bead. Check you are working in a tidy and safe environment, with all the materials you need to hand.

The Mandrel

A mandrel is the metal rod used to hold the bead as it is being worked, and creates a hole in the bead. The mandrel is normally covered in bead release, which later allows the bead to be removed. Mandrels come in a range of diameter sizes.The most readily available sizes are 1/16in (1.6mm), 3/32in (2.4mm) or 3/16in (5mm). The finished diameter of your bead should be at least three times greater than your mandrel size, ensuring that your bead is thick enough to prevent breakage.

To prepare the mandrel, rub fine sandpaper over new mandrels to roughen the surface. This will help the bead release to adhere to the metal. To prolong the life of your bead release, store your pot upside down to keep the bottle airtight. Ensure that your mandrel is clean and dry before you dip one end into the pot of bead release. Hold the mandrel upright, dip into the release and pull it out without touching the pot. Turn the mandrel upright and stand it up in a pot full of either sand or vermiculite to dry.

Most bead release solutions can be dried in the flame just before use, but some need to be dried in the air. Ensure it is dry and intact to prevent moisture penetrating the glass and producing air bubbles, which would have to be removed from the glass.

The torch, tools and materials ready for lampworking.

Coating a mandrel in bead release.

Lighting the Flame

To light your torch, make sure that the taps on your torch are closed and the values on the propane and oxygen tanks are open, or your Oxy-con is turned on. Open the propane tap on at the torch and light the flame with a

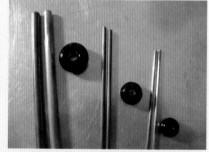
Different sizes of mandrels and donut-shaped beads made in the flame.

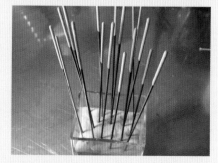
Stand the mandrels up in a pot of sand or vermiculite to dry.

spark device. Adjust the flame to approximately 7in (17.8cm) in length. Slowly turn on the oxygen tap until the cones at the tip of the torch are approximately ¼in–½in (6–8mm) long and well defined in shape. When it is time to turn the torch off, turn the oxygen off first, followed by the propane. Turn off the cylinder values and Oxy-con immediately. (The torch on/off routine is known as POOP – propane, oxygen/oxygen, propane.) The various parts of the flame all play an important part in the lampworking process. The hottest part and one where the melting and heating of your

bead is carried out is at the tip of the blue cone of the flame, approximately 2in (5cm) from the torch. As you move further away from the torch, the flame is slightly cooler and is known as the decorative area, and finally the outer tip is the warming area.

Hold the mandrel between your thumb and forefinger from above and rest the mandrel loosely on your fingers. You should be able to rotate the mandrel in this position to maintain an even-shaped bead. Hold the glass rod between your thumb and forefinger, this time from underneath. Practise this position before making a shaped bead.

Light the flame with a spark device and adjust.

Get used to the correct way of holding the mandrel and glass rod.

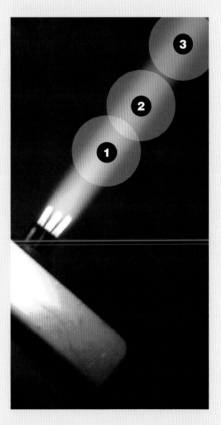

Use different parts of the flame for lampworking:
1. Melting area.
2. Decorative area.
3. Warming area.

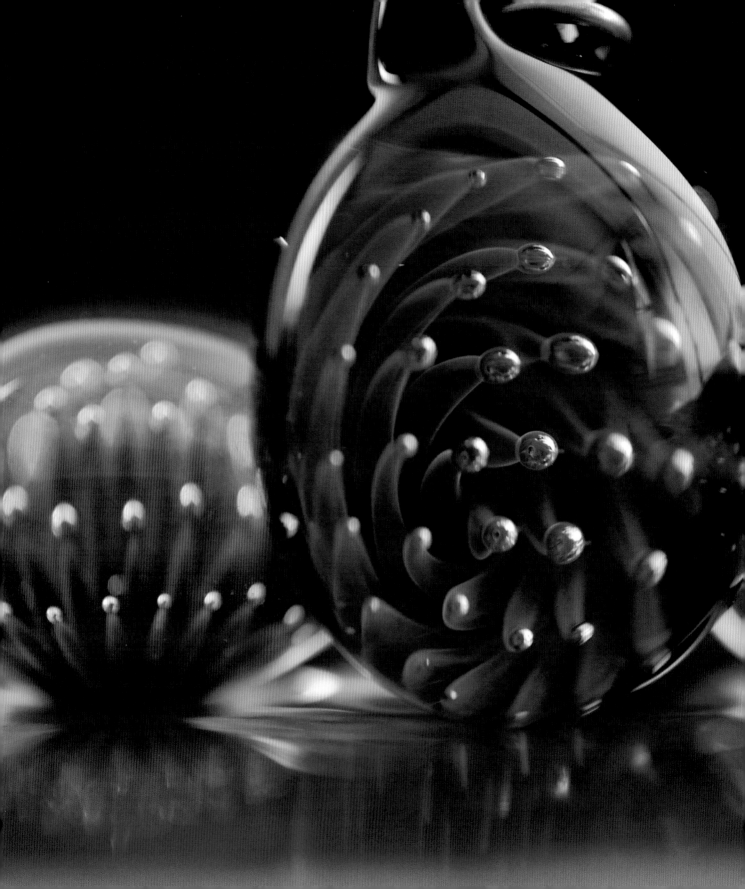

MELTING GLASS

create shapes, textures and hollow beads

In this section professional lampwork artist Lesley Rands will guide you step by step through techniques for melting glass. You will be shown the basics of lampwork from making a bead and creating various shapes to how to use decorative techniques and make them uniquely yours. Making a ring-donut shaped glass bead is the basic foundation of lampwork beads. Time spent learning and perfecting this important technique will set you on the road to creating endless objects of beauty. Once you have mastered such skills you will be ready to try the decorative techniques of the following section.

MAKING A LAMPWORK BEAD

Materials needed

- Prepared mandrels and bead release

Glass rods:

- Donut: Black glass
- Cylinder: Red glass
- Round: Blue glass
- Square: Black glass
- Flat: Purple glass
- Cone: Green glass
- Bicone: Purple glass
- Rod rest
- Jar of water
- Pliers
- Diamond bead reamer
- Marver (hand-held or torch top)
- Flat-nosed tweezers (or mashers)

For all lampworking

- Torch supplied with oxygen and propane
- Spark device for lighting flame
- Safety glasses
- Fibre blanket, kiln or burner

Prepare your work area, tools, materials and mandrels ready for lampwork, as described in the previous chapter. Your first mandrel bead should be a donut-shaped bead made using firm glass such as cobalt blue or transparent black. Once the basic donut shape is mastered, you should be able to try the different shapes in this section and create your own individual designs.

Hold the mandrel in your less dominant hand (your left hand if you are right handed and vice-versa). Now bring your rod of glass slowly into the flame with your right. Any sudden move here will result in unpleasant spitting or breakage of the glass. Waft the rod up and down in the end of the flame to start, then bring the glass in closer to the torch towards the 'melting' area. At the same time, bring your mandrel into the flame behind the glass rod to warm it until you can see a small red glow **A**. This is the point where you want to start making your bead.

Technique Tip

Heat the glass slowly. Heating or cooling glass too quickly may cause it to pop and shatter, so you need to protect your eyes.

Once you have a pea-sized gather of glass on the end of your rod, bring the mandrel in closer to the torch and slightly beneath the flame. Bring your glass rod over to the right of the flame

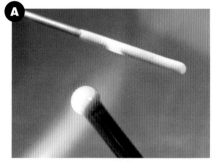

and very lightly touch the mandrel with your gather **B**. Slowly rotate the mandrel until you have a complete circle of glass. You should be working just outside of the flame at this point.

Break off the glass rod by bringing it in closer to the flame and melting the join between the bead and rod **C**. Keep the glass rod at right angles to the mandrel for an even-shaped bead.

Put the glass rod down on the rod rest and your bead back into the melting point of the flame to reheat and shape. Keep the mandrel both horizontal and rotating at the same time. When you are happy with the shape, take the bead out of the flame **D**, rotating until the bead has firmed up.

The first small bead on your mandrel is known as the 'footprint' and its size will vary according to the required size of your final bead **E**. Start with a very small footprint and build up the size with several layers. Bring your bead back into the higher part of the flame to keep it warm. Reheat the glass rod to form a slightly larger gather of glass than before.

Repeat the previous steps by wrapping a second disk of glass around the top of your base bead. Keep the bead in the flame just to the right of the melting area **F**. Rotate the mandrel slowly so that the glass flows over the base bead and increases in size. Apply heat all over the bead, so that the glass shapes and spreads itself out evenly.

If you lose control, take the bead out of the heat **G** and wait for it to cool before starting again.

Keep adding glass until you have a bead of the required size. Your base bead should be firm before you start to add another wrap of glass **H** or else the heat and pressure will distort your bead.

Technique Tip

Check all the safety instructions have been followed when you light your flame (see page 26).

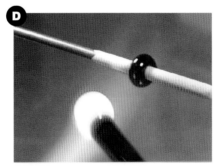

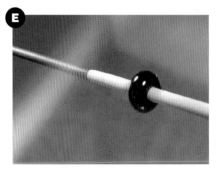

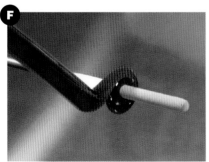

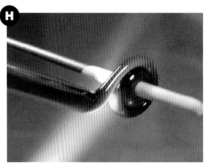

Donut bead

When heating and shaping your bead, particularly if applying decorations later, it is important to apply an even controlled heat onto the glass.

If you have maintained an even-shaped bead so far, the final heating stage should be a quick process. The aim is to have a well-balanced bead with the mandrel directly in the centre 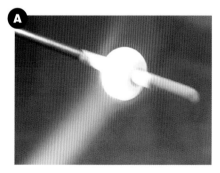 of the bead. The ends of the bead, where it joins the mandrel, should have slight indentations (known as puckers).

Take your bead out of the heat and, whilst rotating, allow it to firm up and form a protective skin, which will maintain the bead's shape. Gently waft the bead in the warming part of the flame giving it time to cool down in the centre whilst keeping the surface warm. The colour **B** will guide you to when the bead is set enough to go into a kiln or fibre blanket.

After your cool bead comes out of the kiln or fibre blanket, place the bead and mandrel into a jar of warm water **C** and leave for as long as possible to soften the bead release. With a pair of pliers, grip the mandrel and gently twist off the bead.

The bead will have a dirty centre with bead release deposits in the mandrel hole. Use water and a specialist diamond bead reamer tool or a clean mandrel to carefully clean the centre of your bead **D**. It is worth the time and effort this takes to produce a quality bead.

Designer Tip

Use the same basic technique to make your bead in different shapes and colours.

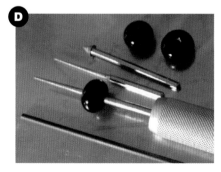

Cylinder bead

When the basic donut shape has been successfully achieved, try some other beads based on the basic shape. This cylinder bead has some tricky beadmaking skills.

Make two equal-sized donut beads to start your cylinder, placing them apart to the desired length of your bead **A**. Keep the first bead warm whilst making the second bead.

Melt one end of your glass rod to a very hot gather and fill the gap between the two beads **B**. Keep the glass hot to avoid trapping air bubbles at the ends. Applying a little pressure, melt the glass until you have filled the gap.

Apply heat to the centre of the glass to shape the cylinder. When molten and smooth, take out of the heat and then very gently begin to roll the bead on a marver **C**. The glass will still be very fluid, so bring the bead and marver together slowly, rotating the mandrel as they meet.

Once the bead is level and nicely shaped, apply heat to each end to round off and shape **D**.

If the ends are uneven, use the edge of the marver to straighten **E** or a pair of flat-nosed tweezers (or mashers) to shape. If you need to add more glass, add a few dots at a time and melt in.

Apply a gentle heat to 'fire polish' your bead to remove any chill marks that may have appeared from coming into contact with the cold marver **F**. Use a doming block to help if necessary. Place the bead in a kiln to anneal.

A

B

C

D

E

F

Round bead

Round beads are the perfect shape for making into bold jewellery designs. They are based on a cylinder shape; and created by forming two disks first.

First make a small blue cylinder-shaped bead **A**. The length of the cylinder should be the required diameter of your finished round bead.

Keeping the cylinder bead warm and held beneath the flame, apply a disk of glass at one end of the cylinder. The disk needs to be slightly higher than the required size of your final bead **B**. Thoroughly warm your bead in the flame before moving to the next step.

Apply a second disk to the other end of your cylinder with exactly the same width and height **C**, taking care to keep the first half of your bead warm to avoid breakage through heat lost.

Bring your bead back into the heat. Position it so that the flame is directed in between the two disks and the mandrel held just beneath the direct heat **D**. The disks will start to soften and fall towards the centre of the bead.

Maintaining the flame in this central position, keep applying heat to the centre of your bead **E** until both sides have fully collapsed. The glass will flow towards the heat.

Take the bead out of the flame and allow it to cool and shape itself, by gravity, into a round shape. Use a doming block to help. Keep rotating the mandrel until firm and the colour returns **F** before annealing in a kiln.

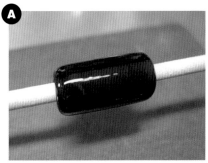

Square bead

Square beads are a variation of the more usual circular beads and have flat surfaces to apply your decorations. To make a square bead, begin with making a round bead.

Make a basic round black bead. Allow the bead to firm up before heating one side only until glowing hot. Bring the bead down on a marver and apply slight pressure  to flatten one side.

Lift up the bead and rotate it by one quarter (90°). Apply heat to this second area. Press down onto a marver to form the second side of your square bead. Continue until all four sides **B** have been flattened.

Repeat the previous step several times until the side edges of the square bead are at right angles to each other to form a cube **C**. Ignore for now the chill marks (circles) made on the sides.

When the sides have been shaped, apply heat to the ends **D**, taking care not to spoil the pucker ends. Parallel mashers may be used in shaping, but the slightest angle away from parallel will distort the final shape.

Using your marver, press the ends of your beads to flatten them **E**. Examine the beads regularly to ensure that the shape is even and well balanced. Correct if necessary.

When the shaping of your bead is finished, allow it to firm up **F** and then 'bathe' in and out of the heat to fire polish out any chill markings created by contact with the cold marver. Place in a kiln for annealing.

Flat disk bead

You should make your flat bead at least three times the thickness (or diameter) of your mandrel. Any thinner than this and your bead is too fragile and in danger of breaking.

Make a purple cylinder. The size of the cylinder should be the required diameter of your final disk bead. Apply a small gather of glass to the cylinder and rotate the mandrel, adding glass to the centre **A** to form a disk.

Apply heat to the centre of your bead until molten **B** but at the same time avoiding the ends becoming so hot that they become drawn to the centre and lose their shape.

Take it out of the heat and allow the glow to fade. Keep rotating the mandrel to keep the glass central and evenly balanced. With the flat-sided mashers, gently squeeze the glass **C** until the bead is the required thickness.

Your bead should need little or no adjustment **D** other than to fire polish to remove any chill marks caused by the cold mashers. Do not overheat or your disk bead will become curved!

A simple adaptation is to make your disk bead into a square. Using the mashers again, squeeze the two outer edges together **E** to form a square shaped bead.

It may be necessary to reshape the flat sides and edges several times to achieve an even shape **F**. Fire polish the bead to remove any chill marks and place your bead in a kiln for annealing.

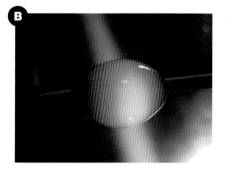

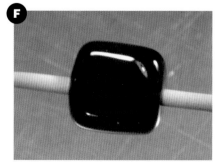

Cone bead

Cone-shaped beads are made from two different-sized donut-shaped beads. Cones are an ideal shape for making earrings or to use on a string of beads in a bracelet or necklace.

Start by making two donut-shaped green beads on your mandrel **A**. The distance apart of the beads forms the total length of your bead between the neck and base.

Fill in the gap between the two beads with glass **B**, tapering the thickness of the glass from the thick to the thin end. When heating, avoid melting the two outer ends of your donut beads to maintain the shape of the puckers.

The shaping of the cone is done in two parts. Take the bead out of the flame and gently marver the thin end of the bead **C** to the desired angle of your cone. Reheat and shape if necessary.

Increase the width of the thicker end of the cone by applying more glass to the base **D**. It will make the next step easier if you try to graduate the thickness slightly towards the thinner end as you start applying heat.

Gradually melt in the additional glass to form an even cone **E**. Avoid distorting the pucker end or heating the top end of the bead as this firmer part will help shape the other end of the cone.

Allow to cool slightly before shaping. Using the marver **F**, shape the thicker end by using the angle already created at the thin end. Reheat and shape the base end. Fire polish to remove chill marks and place in a kiln for annealing.

Bicone bead

Bicone beads are initially created from a cylinder bead. A glass disk is added around the cylinder bead to create the thickness of the bead at the centre. The tapered shape of the bicones is then created by the flow of glass under gravity. Each end of the bead is marvered into shape.

Make a purple cylinder bead, the same length as you want your bicone bead to be. Add a ring of glass to the centre of the cylinder (see page 62) and, while rotating the mandrel, add more rings of glass **A** to form a disk.

Bring your bead back into the flame and apply heat in the first instance to the edge of the ring to melt it down a little **B**. Use a pair of flat-nosed tweezers (or mashers) to keep the circle of glass straight and in position around the cylinder.

When the ring is rounded, change the position of the bead so that the heat is directed at the angle created on one side by the ring. The glass will start to flow towards the heat and create a tapered shape **C**. Avoid heating the cylinder end to maintain its shape.

Technique Tip

Avoid pressing the cone too hard against the marver or you'll make a flat area on the bead.

When fully molten, take the glass out of the flame and marver one end into a cone shape **D**. Hold the mandrel at an angle and, very gently at first, roll backwards and forwards, reheating again if necessary to achieve your required shape, which will be slightly bulbous at this stage.

As the glass cools and becomes harder, apply a little more pressure to your bead when marvering **E**. Continue to reheat and shape until you are happy with the first half of your bicone shape.

Change the angle of your mandrel and bring your bead back into the flame to apply heat to the second end of the bicone shape **F**. Direct the flame at the angle created by marvering the first half.

When fully melted, bring the bead out of the flame, wait for the glow to fade and bring the bead back to the marver to shape into the second half of the bicone shape. The aim is to get your two sides even and meeting in a straight edge at the bead's centre **G**. Reheat and marver the bead until you are happy with the overall shape.

Make final adjustments to the ends of the bead, if necessary **H**. Reheat the area and straighten the edges with your marver. If more glass is required, apply small dots of glass to the bead, reheat and shape.

If you are making a set of bicones, have a sample bead in front of you **I** whilst working to measure the length and width of the bead, and also count the number of additional rings of glass you apply to the centre of the bead to ensure it has a similar thickness. Anneal your bead in the kiln in the usual manner.

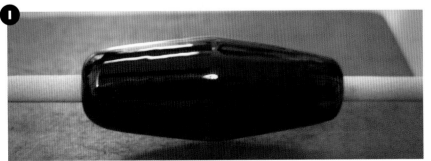

USING A BRASS PRESS

Using a brass press opens up a whole new range of shapes for the beadmaker and allows you to make a set of beads of uniform size. A basic lentil-press has been used here, but the process is virtually the same with other presses.

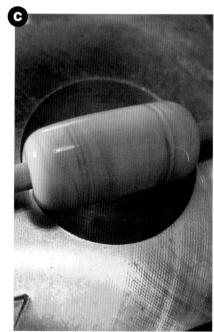

Materials needed

- Prepared mandrel and bead release
- Rod of ivory glass
- Brass lentil-press
- Marver

Before you make your bead, position your press in a safe position **A** to enable you to bring your mandrel to the press and to apply pressure to the top of the press with your other hand.

Select a mandrel with sufficient bead release to cover the lentil-press and lay down a small base donut-shaped bead, which will form the left-hand

edge of your bead. Apply heat to the end of the mandrel and the glass rod. Take the mandrel to the press and lay a small marker dot on the right-hand side **B** to give you the width of your finished bead.

Lay down a second bead to form the right-hand edge and make a basic cylinder-shape bead. Allow the bead to

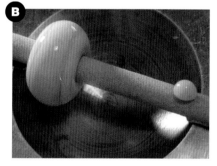

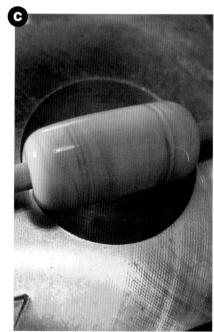

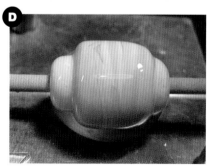

cool and firm up . Make the cylinder bead at least ¹⁄₃₂in (1mm) smaller than your press to allow for excess glass when pressing and to create nicely shaped puckers.

With the shape of your press in mind, continue to add glass to your cylinder bead, so gradually building up the volume . Keep checking your bead against the press to judge the quantity of glass required.

When you have sufficient glass on your mandrel, bring the bead into the flame and apply an all-over heat, ensuring the ends are hot, until the glass is glowing and almost molten . Take it out of the flame and bring to the press.

You can do this next stage in one step if you are confident. However, you may prefer to do it in several parts: first press the glass onto the base of the press. Now quickly turn it over and press the other side down on to the base to help the glass mould into the shape.

Reheat the glass, return to the base and apply the top of the press to your bead. Hold the top of the press down for a maximum of two seconds to avoid thermal shock to the glass and release . You may find that the bead release on the mandrel will break. This will not prevent the release of the bead, but make sure that all loose particles are removed from the press before you use it again.

If you have slightly too much glass, take the bead back into the flame and fire polish the edges. Smooth any excess glass into the body shape.

If you need to add more glass to your bead, add it to the flat, central surface, reheat and re-press . Do not add to the edges. Decorations can be applied before pressing if fully melted in, or after pressing if raised. Anneal in the kiln in the usual manner.

Technique Tip

Brass is a cold metal and will shock the glass when it comes into contact with it. Preheat the press by placing it on top of the kiln prior to use.

SHAPING GLASS WITH TOOLS

A keen lampworker will soon start to accumulate a selection of tools to help shape their glass beads and sculptures. The basics include a marver, a pair of flat-nosed tweezers and some sharp-edged tools. The following techniques use sharp-edged tools, razor tools, tweezers and a pick.

Heart bead

Materials needed

- Prepared mandrel and bead release
- Rod of red glass
- Marver
- Sharp-edged tool

Designer Tip

Make the heart as even shaped as possible. Rework the bead in flame if it loses its shape.

Begin your solid heart bead by making a cone-shaped bead. Apply glass on either side to form 'wings' **A**. Taper them slightly to increase the width at the top of the heart.

Apply more lengths of glass over the 'shoulders' of the bead to create the bulbous feature of the heart **B**. Take care not to touch the mandrel with this additional glass and so keep a nicely shaped pucker on the top of the bead.

Return the bead to the flame but only heat one side at a time to shape **C**. Allow the glass to heat and flow with gravity by changing the direction of the flame. Hold the mandrel at different

angles to allow the glass to flow into the 'shoulders' of the heart and become bulbous.

Allow the first side to firm up before you start heating the second side, or it will distort as you turn it over. The aim is to get both sides symmetrical, so reheat and reshape the bead until you have an even-shaped **D** heart.

Using a sharp-edged tool, make an indentation either side of the mandrel in the centre of the bead **E** to create the characteristic heart shape.

Adjust the shape of the heart, depending on your preference **F**. Decorate as required and place in a kiln for annealing.

Melon bead

This melon bead is a bicone-shaped bead with lengthwise indentations made with a single-edged razor tool.

Materials needed

- Prepared mandrel and bead release
- Rod of purple glass
- Marver
- Single-edged razor tool

Make a small bicone bead and use the heat of the flame to round off the centre into a bulbous shape **A**.

Technique Tip

If the ends become pointed during heating, cool off the bead, reheat one half and then hold the mandrel upright. The glass will flow back to the end of the bead.

Using a single-edged razor tool, make an indentation from one end to the other, running parallel with the mandrel. Make a one-quarter turn away from you (i.e. 90°) and make a second indentation in the bead. Repeat until you have four lines **B** that mark your bead into quarters.

Continue adding lines in the gaps until you are happy with the design **C**. Fire polish to finish your bead. Add any decorations to the bead as required and anneal the bead in the kiln.

Spiral-striped bead

Wrap a cylinder bead in a stringer (see page 66), a long piece of pulled glass used for decoration. A single-edged razor is applied to give an unusual zigzag pattern.

Materials needed

- Prepared mandrel and bead release
- Rod of white glass
- Black stringer
- Single-edged razor
- Marver

Make a white cylinder bead. Hold the black stringer at right angles to the bead. Turn the bead to create a spiral 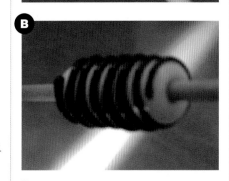 pattern along the bead.

Take the spiral back to the flame **B**. Secure and finish the ends and flash heat along both sides to secure to the bead. Melt the stringer in flat with the bead and reshape if necessary.

Allow to firm up and then reheat one length of the bead to soften the surface. Using a single-edged razor, move the glass in one direction to create a 'V' shape in four equally spaced lines **C** around the bead. In between each line reheat and repeat the process in the opposite direction to create a zigzag pattern. Anneal in a kiln.

Daisy bead

This bead in the shape of a flower is manipulated using scissors and some tweezers. A number of these beads could be strung onto a necklace to make up a design.

Materials needed

- Rod of transparent purple glass
- Rod of opaque glass
- Glass scissors
- Pair of tweezers

A simple donut bead forms the centre of the flower, by creating a disk of glass wound around the centre. A slightly darker shade of glass is used for the outer ring to add depth. Spot-heat one small area of the disk on both sides and use a pair of glass scissors **A** to snip the glass to make the petals.

Taking care not to cut or mark the central base bead, continue heating and cutting the outer disk to make all the petals **B** of the daisy flower. The individual petals may well become slightly twisted from the heat, so use a pair of tweezers to straighten them back into place.

Continue to surface heat and shape each of the petals to make a daisy flower **C**. The tweezer marks add texture to the petals and can be left or carefully fire polished out. Anneal in the kiln in the usual manner.

Dragged heart

Dots are applied by melting the tip of a glass rod onto a bead (see page 79) to create a dome. If dots are melted flush with the glass, the dragging technique can be used.

Materials needed

- Prepared mandrel and bead release
- Rod of red glass
- Rod of white glass
- Rod of black glass
- Pick

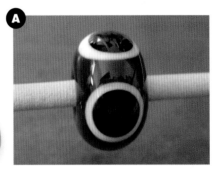

Make a small donut bead with the red glass. Apply the first layer of dots in white, and melt them in flush with the bead. Add smaller black dots. Leave spaces in between the placed dots to allow for dragging. Allow the bead **A** to firm up completely.

Hold the mandrel so that the base of your bead is in the flame and turn the bead away from you so that the glowing part comes up to the top. Using only the very tip of your pick, break the surface of the pattern and rotate the bead so that the glowing glass comes out of the flame and the pick drags the dots **B** into heart shapes.

The bead will have tramlines in it after dragging, so return to the heat and melt flush again. Experiment with different pointed tools and dot designs **C**. Anneal in the kiln in the usual manner.

TEXTURED BEADS

Textured beads are fun to make and can give you some really funky designs. The ribbed effect was bought from a glass supplier, the circular sheet was from an engineering workshop and the sea creatures from a picture frame found at a car boot sale!

Ribbed sheet

Materials needed

- Prepared mandrel and bead release
- Rod in red or clear glass
- Ribbed plate

Collect some interesting textures 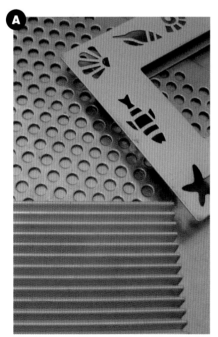 **A** that you can use for making beads, including ribbed plate.

For a ribbed effect bead make a cylinder bead. Allow the bead to firm up fully whilst keeping it warm in the tip of the flame. Reheat only the outer surface **B** and keep the centre stiff to avoid distortion of the whole bead.

Take the bead out of the flame and before the surface cools, take the bead to the ribbed textured plate. Holding the bead at a 45° angle to the grooves **C**, roll the bead in one continuous forward movement until the ribs form a complete pattern. Apply enough pressure to pick up the pattern, without distorting the bead. Work quickly, while the bead is hot.

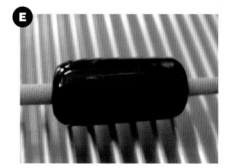

Lift the bead from the plate and check the pattern has picked up evenly . Fire polish the bead to remove any chill marks that it will have picked up from the coldness of the metal.

You can experiment with different effects and find the one that suits your bead best. For a horizontal ribbed bead, follow the steps above, but turn the mandrel so that it is at a 90° angle **E** to the ribs of the metal.

Keep the bead perfectly straight whilst you roll **F** on the texture to ensure the lines meet up after each revolution. These beads can be decorated or left plain as required. Anneal the beads in a kiln in the usual manner.

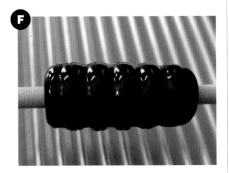

Technique Tip

You can add textured coatings to beads by applying enamels to the surface for interesting effects.

Textured sheet

This creates a similar bead to the ribbed bead, but by using a flat textured metal sheet and a photo frame with cut-out designs to create varied patterns for beads. The only limit for creating interesting textures is your imagination.

Materials needed

- Prepared mandrels and bead release
- Rod of ivory glass
- Rod of blue glass
- Textured metal sheet
- Metal picture frame

Make a flat disk bead in blue and allow to firm up and cool a little before heating one side only **A** to a glow.

Press down firmly onto a patterned surface. Turn the bead over **B** and repeat on the opposite side. Fire polish any chill marks from the bead.

To add a texture or design, any non-combustible metal surface can be used. An old photograph frame was used to make this starfish **C** pattern in ivory glass. Anneal in a kiln in the usual manner.

HOLLOW BEADS

To make a hollow bead, two glass disks are created in a continuous spiral on the mandrel and 'knitted' together to create a bead with a firm surface. Be careful not to create any holes in the bead, which will cause it to collapse.

Materials needed

- Rods in clear and/or transparent green glass
- Prepared mandrel and bead release
- Flat-nosed tweezers (or mashers)
- Doming block (optional)

Melt a small gather of glass and make a small footprint wrap on your mandrel. With your mandrel placed directly below the flame and your rod placed directly in the flame, add glass from the rod **A** in a continuous spiral.

Use flat-nose tweezers (or mashers) to help straighten your disk if it is curved. If the rod breaks off before you have finished, warm up your disk in the higher part of the flame **B** and then rejoin and add more glass from where you finished.

Make a second disk, parallel to the first one and the same height. To keep the first disk warm, either break off the rod in the flame and re-warm the first disk **C** or move your mandrel into the warming part of the flame occasionally, whilst holding the rod of glass steady.

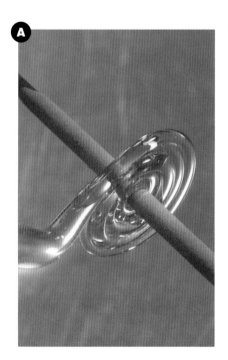

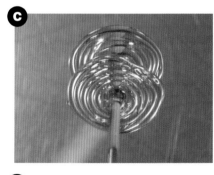

Apply glass to the inside edge of each disk to gradually bridge the gap in between the two. Continue wrapping the glass on each side **D** until the gap remaining is approximately ⅛in–¼in (3–6mm) wide. Take time to heat both discs at regular intervals to prevent cooling and breakage.

Bring the bead back into the flame and warm thoroughly. Direct the heat onto the two edges of the discs in the centre and when glowing red, take the glass rod and 'knit' the two sides together **E** in a left to right motion.

The bead is now in one piece and is ready for the final stage **F**. The critical point now is that there should be no holes in your glass, which would allow

air to escape and result in the bead collapsing. Keeping the bead warm at all times. Check and apply dabs of glass to any remaining holes.

Apply heat to the centre of your bead to smooth and shape the surface but also to heat the air inside **G**. The bead will appear to shrink slightly at first before the air inside the glass expands. If any holes are left in your bead at this stage, the glass will collapse onto the mandrel and your bead will have failed on this occasion.

Continue heating the entire bead, paying attention to both ends to form neat puckers at the mandrel **H**. The bead may become unstable as it is heated, so bring it out of the flame to

cool slightly and reshape as necessary. A brass doming block can be useful for doing this.

After shaping is completed **I**, allow the bead to firm up before placing it in the kiln for annealing. To clean the bead, fill it with water and then blow into the bead through the end to force the bead release (and the water) out of the other end.

Technique Tip

A small dot of glass may be placed on the end of the mandrel to count the number of rotations made to keep the two sides even.

Hollow heart bead

Hollow heart-shaped beads are made from a standard round hollow bead. Be careful not to make the hollow bead too wide or allow the glass to become too thin. You will be manipulating the surface to make the heart shape.

Materials needed

- Prepared mandrel and bead release
- Rods of green glass
- Decorative enamel
- Sharp-edged tool
- Marver

Technique Tip

Mandrel preparation is important with hollow beads, as there is only a small area of the glass in contact with the mandrel. Any pressure applied to the bead in progress may lead to the breakage of the bead release.

Make a round hollow bead and allow the bead to firm up. Apply a dusting of enamel to give your bead added interest **A**. Enamel powders are very fine particles of ground glass, used to add decorative effects.

Shape the heart by applying heat to one half of the bead only **B**. Do not overheat the glass at this stage or the bead may burst if the glass is too thin.

A

B

C

Take the bead away from the heat and, using a sharp-edged tool, make a crease in the top of the bead to form the lobes at the top of the heart **C**. Use the tool to shape both the front and the back crease, widening the crease if need be. If the bead becomes stiff whilst shaping, take it back to the flame and carefully reheat.

To shape the base of the heart, apply heat to the bottom of the bead until it is glowing, but not fluid. Take a rod of the same colour as the bead and briefly warm the tip of the rod. Working very quickly, before the glass cools, attach a pulling rod (the punty) to the base of the heart by pushing it gently onto the central base point **D** of the bead.

With a steady hand, very gently pull the rod towards you **E**. The glass will cool quickly. It is very tricky to reheat the bead at this stage, so make sure your glass is hot before you start to pull.

Take the bead back into the flame to burn off the pulling rod, which should come away quite easily and make any adjustments to the shape as necessary (see page 62) **F**. Place in the kiln to anneal in the usual manner.

Technique Tip

Take extra time to achieve smooth puckers at the mandrel, which will improve the finished shape of the heart.

Designer Tip

Hollow beads are extremely light. They are useful for making necklaces that would be too heavy if made with solid beads.

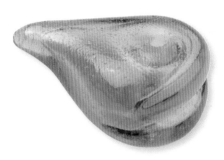

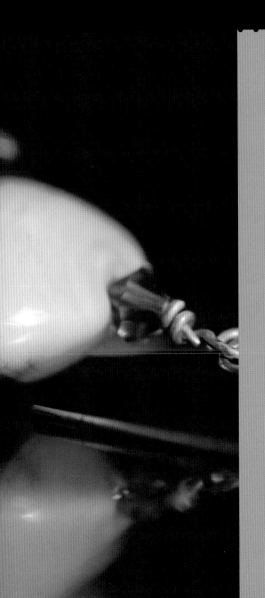

DECORATIVE TECHNIQUES
create dots, lines, twists and flowers

In this section Lesley Rands shows you a range of decorative techniques to apply to lampwork. Most are based around the use of a stringer – the long thin piece of glass that is used to create decorative patterns on a lampwork bead or melted glass. Stringers open up an endless range of decorative techniques. They are used to create dots, lines, twisted patterns and flowers on the surface of a bead. They can also be used when making sculptured images where the delicate addition of very small amounts of glass is required. They can be further manipulated using a variety of tools to form stunning effects.

BASIC STRINGERS

Stringers are long pieces of glass used to create decorative patterns on lampwork. When you start to decorate your beads you will need a selection of stringers of different colours, types and thicknesses. The variations and types are endless.

Materials needed

- Glass rods
- Flat-nosed tweezers (or pliers)
- Disk (or glass rod) cutters

Make a basic stringer in one colour by melting a small gather of glass at the end of your rod **A**.

Take the glass out of the flame and move over to your working area to the side of your torch. With a pair of flat-nosed tweezers (or pliers), pinch a very small edge of the gather to obtain a 'handle' to pull the glass **B**. Allow the glass to cool slightly first.

Keeping your hands parallel, move them apart with the tweezer hand, keeping control of the pulling action **C**. The required thickness of the finished stringer will depend on how fast and how thin you pull the glass. When the glass has cooled, either break off the stringer with a pair of disk (or glass rod) cutters or apply pressure with your tweezers or fingers to snap the stringer away.

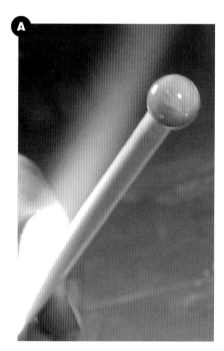

This is an alternative method of pulling the glass into a stringer. It gives the same results but is preferred by many people when doing very fine work. It involves using two rods of the same glass. To begin with, melt both ends in the flame at the same time **D**.

When both ends have a molten glow, bring them out of the flame and push the two pieces together **E**. Bring back into the flame and with a slight inward pressure melt the join until you have a small gather of glass at the centre.

Bring the glass rods out of the flame and gently open up the gather by pulling your two hands apart **F**. Cut your stringer away from the glass rods as described earlier.

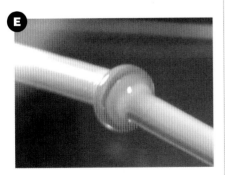

Silver-leaf stringer

This stringer guarantees to provide you with some lovely effects on your beads using silver leaf.

Materials needed

- Silver leaf
- Rod of ivory glass
- Marver

Fold a quarter sheet of silver leaf in half and lay on a marver **A**. Heat a small gather of dark ivory, opaque glass.

Allow your gather to firm up and roll the glass onto the silver leaf **B**. The silver will adhere easily to the glass, but apply slight pressure to the marver with the glass to ensure that the leaf has made contact with the whole area.

Heat the silvered gather as you would for a basic stringer **C**. The metallic element of the gather tends to make your string a little more 'lumpy', so allow heat to penetrate fully into the centre before you start to pull with your tweezers. Cut away your stringer.

Technique Tip

Keep the size of your gather small in order to keep control of your final stringer.

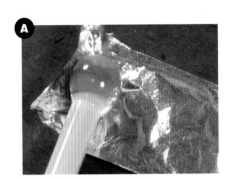

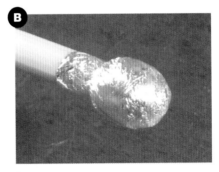

ENCASED STRINGERS

This stringer is made by using transparent glass to encase goldstone. Goldstone is a brown glass flecked with copper particles. It burns easily in a flame, so is protected by encasing it (see page 89) before being pulled into a stringer.

Materials needed

- Goldstone (gold aventurine)
- Glass rods
- Pair of flat-nosed pliers (or mashers)
- Glass rod cutters
- Marver

Choose a small chunk of goldstone to encase in glass. Melt the end of a clear glass rod into a flat disk **A**.

Heat the disk until glowing and press down onto the goldstone chunk. Place the glass rod near the end of the flame and very gently begin to heat the stone **B**. It will start to glow and melt. More stone may be added, although it is best to keep the gather fairly small.

Shape the gather ready to encase with clear glass **C**. The shape should not allow the glass to trap air bubbles. You can use a pair of small flat-nosed pliers (or mashers) to shape the gather.

Encase the goldstone in clear glass. Keep the neck of the glass rod away from the heat as it may droop if too much heat is applied. One or two layers of glass should be applied **D**.

A

B

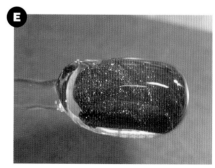

C

D

E

The gather now needs to be heated to melt the encasing glass and to ensure that the goldstone is hot enough to pull into a stringer. Heat in several stages by taking out of the flame to allow the surface to cool a little **E**, but for the heat to radiate to the centre.

Attach the second glass rod to the end of the gather and heat until the gather is fluid enough to begin pulling your stringer **F**. Pull your hands apart applying a slow, even tension. Cut your stringer away from the glass rods as previously described.

Technique Tip

Don't add too much goldstone or the gather may become too large.

Filigrana wrapped glass

A white rod encased with a red striking glass produces a beautiful pink stringer of filigrana glass (a clear glass around a thread of colour).

Materials needed

- Rod of white glass
- Rod of red striking glass (Rubino Ora)
- Rod of clear glass

Warm the white (core) rod in the end of the flame. Melt a gather at the end of the red (encasing) rod and touch down with it onto the white rod. The encasing rod should remain in the flame to provide a supply of glass **A** as you wrap the glass around the core rod. The core rod should remain in the cooler area below the flame.

Apply one or two coats of encasing glass **B**, depending on the thickness and depth of colour that you want for your stringer.

Finish the stringer as was previously described, by applying a punty handle of clear glass to the end of the melted gather **C** and pulling the stringer to the desired thickness. Cut your stringer away from the glass rod as previously described.

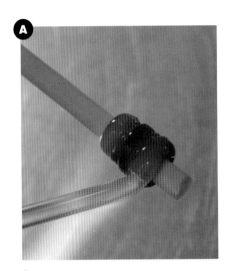

DECORATIVE STRINGERS

There are many types of decorative stringer. A twisty entwines multiple coloured rods to make a stringer. The sunburst stringer makes a chunky stringer that can later be cut into slices of cane and used for decoration. You'll be surprised how easy decorative stringers are to do once you have had some practice.

Twistie

Materials needed

- Glass rods in three colours
- Glass (or mosaic) cutters
- Clear glass rods

To make a tri-coloured twistie, select three coloured rods. Using the first two rods **A**, heat just one side of each rod until the glass begins to glow.

Join the hot sides together. Cut the top rod off level with the end of the bottom rod, with a pair of glass (or mosaic) cutters **B**. Spot heat the third rod of glass on one side and place between the first two rods, aligning the ends. Cut this third rod off level with the first two.

Prepare and attach a punty handle of clear glass to the centre of the cluster of three rods of glass. Using the glass (or mosaic) cutters, change hands and cut off the length of the remaining coloured rod **C**.

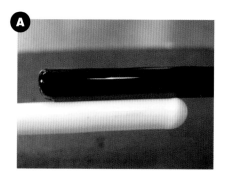

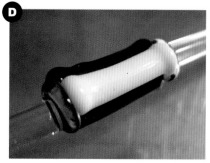

Attach a second punty handle to the end so that the three rods are held firmly and begin to heat the glass rods until the glass begins to fuse together **D**. The handles need to remain firm throughout the heating process, so avoid bringing them into contact with the flame.

Continue heating the gather until it reaches the very fluid and molten stage. It may be difficult to control it at this stage so push the two punty handles slightly together **E** to regain control. Take out of the flame and wait for around five seconds so the gather has time to stabilise.

Slowly begin to rotate the two punty handles in opposite directions to start twisting the gather. Whilst twisting, very gradually pull the two punty ends apart to stretch the twistie into a stringer **F**. Work quickly and evenly as the glass begins to cool. The twistie can now be used for decorating glass.

Technique Tip

The horizontal cross section of a thick pulled stringer is called cane. It contains the same pattern all the way through. The sunburst stringer is ideal to make into a thick cane. Choose contrasting colours for the bead and stringer and encase the cane in clear glass after it has been completed.

Sunburst stringer

The 'sunburst stringer' is a useful technique to learn. Once you have practised the technique, you can adapt the colours to make thick stringers into decorative cane.

Materials needed

- Rod (ivory) and stringer
- Mashers
- Single-edged razor tool
- Flat-nosed tweezers

Technique Tip

Choose contrasting colours for the rod and stringer.

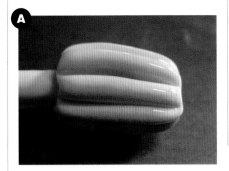

Melt a large gather at the end of your rod and shape into a chunky cylinder with mashers. With a single-bladed razor tool (or similar), make at least eight grooves in the surface **A**.

With a different colour stringer, fill the grooves of the cylinder. Take the ends of the stringer over both ends and secure to the glass by pressing down with a pair of small flat-nosed tweezers to avoid the stringer breaking away **B**. Keep rotating it in the flame to keep all parts warm whilst working.

Pull the stringer by heating the gather **C** and applying a punty as previously described. Leave the stringer slightly thicker if you wish to use it as a cane decoration.

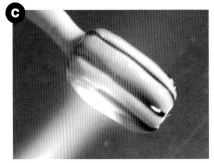

STRINGER CONTROL

You can use a stringer to decorate a base bead by heating the surface so the stringer attaches to it. The stringer is either left raised or melted into the glass. To make fine lines you will need to make very fine stringers, as they expand when melted.

Materials needed

- Prepared mandrel and bead release
- Rod in turquoise glass
- White stringer
- Jar of water
- Flat-nosed tweezers

Make a base bead using the turquoise glass. Allow to cool and firm up. Heat the surface of the bead so that the stringer will attach to it. If the bead is too soft, the stringer will sink. Find the ideal spot in the flame where the stringer will become pliable enough to draw a design, but not hot enough to melt. **A**. Once you have found this spot, the stringer stays here and the bead moves.

Make sure that your stringer has a straight end before you start, by heating the end of the stringer and plunging the tip into a jar of water. Bring your bead and stringer under the flame. To draw a line, bring the stringer down onto the bead and, with a very slight pressure **B**, start to apply the stringer to the bead and at the same time move the bead under the flame in the opposite direction.

A

B

C

D

E

F

As soon as you reach the end of your line, quickly pull the stringer and bead closer to the flame to burn the stringer off **C**. Depending on how secure the line is on your bead, the ends tend to ball slightly with the heat. In order to prevent this, flatten both ends with a pair of tweezers.

To remove surplus glass at the end of the line, heat up the excess glass and, with a cold stringer, pick up the hot glass and pull it away from the bead **D**. Repeat if necessary. When you have finished, flatten down the end as described in the previous step.

You can still move your line slightly if you need to adjust it. Flash-heat the line and use a pair of tweezers to adjust the line **E**. Then, either melt the line flush into the bead or, if you are leaving it raised, flash-heat along both sides to secure it firmly to the surface of the bead.

Once you have mastered drawing lines the next step is to start drawing circular designs and shapes **F**. You must move your bead in different directions whilst drawing with the stringer, so the stringer stays still and the bead moves.

Technique Tip

The place to draw your stringer can be found in the outer edges of the flame, approximately 4in (10cm) from the torch.

Striped stringer bead

This bead is an ideal 'starter' bead for stringer control. Use the same colour base bead and stringer, with a contrast colour wrap over the base bead.

Materials needed

- Prepared mandrel with bead release
- Black bead with white wrap
- Black stringer

Starting at one end, close to but not touching the mandrel, warm the bead and apply a straight line from one side to the other. Secure and adjust the ends. Run the flame over both sides of the finished line to secure **A**. Rotate your bead a quarter turn (90°) towards you and apply a second line.

Repeat the lines until you have three and then four lines **B**. Now fill in between these lines until you have eight lines in total. Keep both the bead and the stringer lines warm so that they don't break away from the surface if they get cold or when they go back into the flame.

Gradually melt the lines into the bead and continue to decorate it **C** as required.

DECORATION WITH STRINGERS

This technique will produce a bead that represents the seashore, using four different stringers as decoration. It is an excellent way to practise your stringer pulling and application.

Materials needed

- Brass lentil-press
- Rod in dark ivory glass
- Rod in light turquoise transparent glass
- Rod in dark blue transparent glass
- Silver ivory stringer (prepared)
- Stringer in light turquoise and white enamel (prepared)
- Sunburst stringer in small slices (prepared)
- Basic black stringer (prepared)
- Flat-nosed tweezers (or pliers)

Technique Tip

If you have problems breaking the stringer when twisting glass, the base bead may be too hot. Try blowing gently on the join and applying a little pressure to break the stringer away.

Prepare a basic raised disk bead (lentil bead) using a brass press to represent the seashore. One end is in dark ivory (beach), the middle is in light turquoise (sea) and the other end in dark blue (sky) 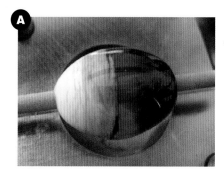. The gather should be slightly smaller than the final size of your bead.

Using a length of silver ivory stringer, apply a line along the top of the dark ivory segment to form a pebble or seaweed effect. With the turquoise and white enamel stringer, apply a heavy band along the central sea section of the bead to create the band of waves and surf .

Reheat the gather and finish your lentil bead by using the lentil-press . If you don't have a lentil-press, adapt the bead to either a large cylinder shape or a flat disk bead.

To create the rolling waves, spot-heat the surface area of the turquoise sea. Using the thick end of the enamel stringer, plunge into the hot glass and twist half a turn (180°) in a clockwise direction **D**. Wait a few seconds for the glass to set and cool, and then 'wiggle' the stringer to snap off at the join with the bead.

Repeat the previous step until you have sufficient waves on both sides of the bead. The surface will become uneven with the twisting action but this is part of the design of the bead. Spot-heat a small area of glass on the beach section for your shell **E**.

Pick up a ⅛in (3mm) slice of the sunburst stringer and then push it firmly into the hot glass **F**. To avoid 'shocking' the sunburst slice, warm it in the flame using the tweezers (or pliers) before placing it onto your bead.

Gently warm the sunburst slice to 'round off' the edges and to secure firmly into the bead. The slice can be fully melted in if you prefer, or left slightly raised. Take the basic black stringer, plunge it into the centre of the slice **G** to form the 'sunburst' effect.

Break off the stringer and repeat the two previous steps on the opposite side of the bead **H**. Apply a warming heat to the whole bead to finish off and place the bead in the kiln for the annealing process.

Designer Tip

Slices of the sunburst stringer are also useful when doing floral decorations on beads.

D

E

G

F

H

DECORATIVE DOTS

Being able to place dots on a bead opens a wide range of possibilities. For different sizes of dot you will need to vary the size of your rods or use hand-pulled stringers of varying thickness. Try out layered dots, twisted dots and poked dots.

Raised dots

Materials needed

- Prepared mandrel and bead release
- Rod in dark green glass
- Rod in white glass
- White stringer

Prepare a basic dark green bead and keep it warm in the tip of the flame. Melt the tip of the white rod. Bring the bead to the flame and, with the glass rod at right angles to the bead, press down with the rod onto the bead **A**. Lift the rod upwards and bring the bead back into the flame to melt the rod from the dot. 'Flash' the dot backwards and forwards in the flame to form an even domed shape.

The dot should have a large round 'footprint' on the base bead and be nicely rounded. You may also find it useful to place a small dot on the mandrel **B** in line with your first dot, which you can use to help when placing subsequent dots on your bead.

To make a bead with four dots around the circumference, turn your bead one quarter turn (90°) towards you so that

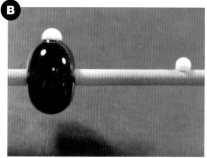

Technique Tip

To reduce your dot, melt it until it just starts to glow red. With a 'cold' rod, or stringer, pick up the surplus glass and pull it away. Burn off any trails of glass.

your first dot is facing you. Repeat the process to secure your second dot. Repeat to make four dots **C**. Warm your bead after each dot has been added.

Dots can be added in a countless number of designs and colours. You could add further dots in the spaces around the bead to give you 12 dots **D**. When completing a pattern with your dots, keep checking your dots are even.

When placing dots at the end of the bead, it may help to change the position of the mandrel in your hand to achieve a right angle with your glass rod **E**. Likewise at the opposite end, change position again and hold the mandrel upright.

For small dots, the process is exactly the same, only quicker. Heat just the very tip of a thin stringer until it is glowing red and forms a small ball **F**. Very quickly apply your dots, pull up to the flame and burn the stringer free. Flash-heat the dot to shape and secure to the base bead.

Layered dots

These dots are melted flush with the surface of your bead and layers are added in an alternating pattern.

Start with a simple black base bead and add four medium-sized white dots around the centre. Return the bead to the flame and evenly reheat the bead. When the dots have melted flush with the surface, take the bead out of the flame and allow to cool slightly until the whites of the dots **A** are visible.

Using alternating colours, apply a slightly smaller black dot in the centre of each white dot **B**. Once again apply an even, all-round heat to melt.

Repeat the steps until you have achieved your required pattern or design and the layers have melted flush **C** with the bead.

Technique Tip

You must allow enough space between the dots for spreading and also apply an even heat to the whole bead so that the dots and the surrounding glass all melt evenly.

Materials needed

- Prepared mandrel and bead release
- Rods in black and white glass

Layered fish scales

A clever use of layered dots and colours makes this colourful design, which can be adapted with any colours or shape of bead.

Materials needed

- Prepared mandrel and bead release
- Rod in dark red glass
- Rod in white glass
- Rod in orange glass
- Rod in yellow glass
- Marver

Make a cylindrical bead in dark red glass. Apply a row of large white base dots around the end of the bead and melt them flush with the bead. Apply a second layer of slightly smaller orange dots **(A)** over the white dots. It doesn't matter how many dots are laid so long as they keep their shape.

Allowing the bead to firm up after each melting, apply a second row of white followed by yellow dots in the gaps of the first row **(B)**. The bead may become a little distorted by the extra glass, but this will even out.

Add a row of white and orange, then continue adding rows of dots until your bead is covered. Shape the bead using a marver **(C)**, taking care not to apply too much pressure when you do this as the pattern may become distorted. Place the bead in the kiln for annealing in the normal manner.

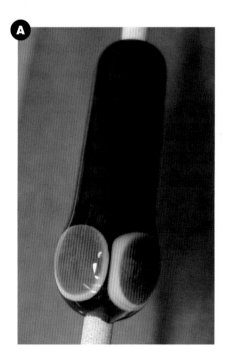

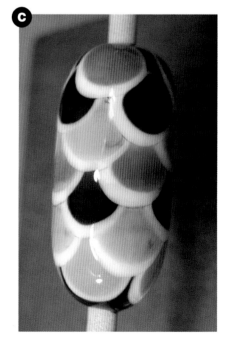

Twisted dots

Twisted dots look difficult to make but, in fact, they are one of the easiest designs to master. Use a stringer to twist the dots into a different shape.

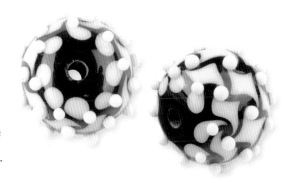

Materials needed

- Prepared mandrel and bead release
- Rod in transparent cobalt blue
- Marver
- Thick 'twisting' stringer in cobalt blue
- Rod or stringer in white

Make a round bead in blue, ³⁄₈in (15mm) in diameter. Apply eight dots around the circumference and two rows of eight slightly smaller dots  to each side.

The bead needs to be firm so it does not distort under pressure. Heat the area between two dots on the centre row. Take the bead out of the heat and rest on marver. With a short, thick stringer of the base colour, plunge into the surface of the bead and twist in a clockwise direction **B** for a half turn (180°). Allow the bead to cool and wiggle the stringer until it snaps off at the surface of the bead. Take the

bead back into the flame and warm thoroughly. Repeat this process until all the dots on the central row have been twisted. Take care to twist all the dots in the same direction to create an even design.

You may prefer to finish your bead at this point, or you can continue twisting between the dots on the remaining rows. To help break off the twisting stringer, blow a puff of air on the join

to cool the stringer first. When you have finished twisting, reheat the bead to melt the surface flush. Make the final adjustments **C** to the shape of the bead.

Complete your bead by applying small raised dots for decoration in the many spaces that you twisted **D**. Flash-heat to secure the dots to the bead and put your bead in the kiln for annealing in the usual manner.

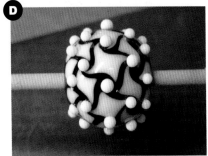

Poked dots

Poked dots are fun to make and will make your bead sparkle as the light catches the tiny bubble of air that is trapped in the glass. Use either in a uniform or random pattern on a floral or abstract design. You will need a 'poking tool' to push down into your bead to form small indentations.

Materials needed

- Prepared mandrel and bead release
- Rods in transparent dark and light green, white and clear glass
- Poking tool
- Marver

Make a green bead and apply four white dots around the centre and another four slightly smaller white dots in the gaps on both sides **A**. Take time to examine your dots to see if they are all the same size. Correct if necessary. The dots are now melted in flush with the surface. The aim is to keep the dots in tight circles and to prevent them from touching each other.

To do this, apply a slow, controlled heat to the whole bead paying attention to both ends **B**. The glass needs to heat evenly to allow the dots to spread at an even rate and so stay in shape.

Once the dots have been melted flush, take the bead out of the flame, still rotating the mandrel, to cool and let the bead harden and become stiff. Apply a

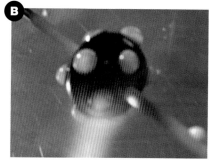

second dot to the centre of your base dots **C** in contrasting transparent green. Melt the contrasting dot in flush with the surface, applying an all-round even heat to maintain your round dots.

Finally, apply a very small clear dot in the centre **D**. This is a small trick that will make your bubble look as if it is floating in air.

Melt the dots in so they are flush **E**. The bead now needs to cool and firm up so that when pressure is applied to the bead during poking, it will not become out of shape and distorted.

Apply heat to one dot at a time during the poking process. The heat should allow the dot to glow red and the colour of the dots to disappear. Bring out of the heat and rest the end of the mandrel on the marver. With the poking tool ready, wait until the colour of the dot appears and plunge the tool into the centre **F**. Continue heating and poking each dot on your bead.

If the heat is correct you should be able to make an indentation of approximately 1/8in (3mm) **G**. If you poke the dot before the colour returns, you may break through the skin of the dot and expose the base glass underneath. This will give a different effect to your bead.

Using a clear rod, apply a dot of glass over each bubble. The trick here is to melt just the very end of the rod and then press down firmly on the bead to cover the whole dot **H**. You might start to see your bubble at this stage.

Finally, melt in the clear layer and display your beautiful bubbles 'suspended' in air **I**. Make any final adjustment to the shape of your bead and place in a kiln for annealing.

Technique Tip

Poking tools can include metal picks, graphite pencils and a double-ended brass rod. The rod includes a sharp end that can be used for making bubbles.

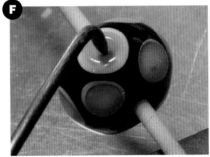

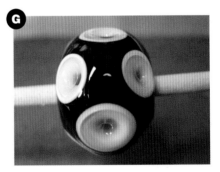

FRITS

Frits are decorations that are used to create colours and patterns on beads. Frit is available in varying sizes, from fine particles to chunks, which is then reduced and broken down. Here are some ideas for decorating with frits.

Materials needed

- Frit (CoE compatible)
- Marver
- Prepared mandrel and bead release
- Rod of white glass
- Stringer
- Rod of clear glass (optional)
- Pointed tool
- Goldstone
- Glass crusher (or hammer)
- Reduction frit

Lay a small quantity of frit on a surface, such as a marver, ready for rolling. Consider the size of the frit and how well you want to cover the bead. Make an opaque white cylinder bead and allow to firm up so that it maintains its shape when rolled **A** in the frit.

Reheat the surface of your bead until it just begins to glow and roll in the frit. Examine the bead, reheat and re-roll as necessary. When ready, return to the flame and begin to melt the frit flush **B** with your bead.

When fully melted, reshape as necessary and continue with your decoration **C**. Encasing the frit bead in clear glass will magnify the frit for a special effect. Before you do this, see if you wish to try the next technique.

Technique Tip

When buying frit, try to buy the correct CoE glass. If using non-compatible CoE frit, only cover about 10 per cent of the surface to prevent cracking when cooled.

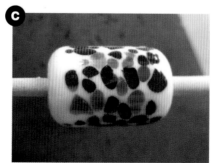

An alternative decorative technique is to either twist your frit using a thick stringer or to drag the surface using a stringer or a pointed tool **D**.

Goldstone can be used as frit but you will need to break down the chunks into frit by using a glass crusher (or hammer). Use a gentle heat when melting goldstone into the bead **E** to prevent the stone from burning.

Reduction frit can produce some special metallic effects. Melt in the frit in a flame, allow the bead to cool until the colour begins to return. Turn up the propane slightly and waft the bead in and out of the tip of the flame, until the glass reacts and you have the desired effect **F**.

Stringers with frit

Reduction frit can also be used to make stringers for bead decoration. They are normally used for raised decoration (including small dots) as they tend to lose their effectiveness when melted in.

Materials needed

- Frit in iris gold
- Metal reservoir
- Rod of clear glass
- Tweezers

Place the iris gold frit in a heat-proof reservoir **A** ready for use with a rod of clear glass.

Melt a pea-sized gather of glass on your rod and quickly roll in the reservoir of frit, pressing down to pick up as much of the frit as possible **B**.

Return the gather to the flame and melt the frit into the surface **C**. Reheat and roll the gather into the frit several times to increase the coverage. Pull into a stringer and use as required.

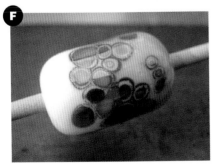

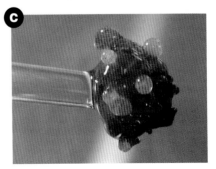

ENAMELS

Enamel powders are very fine particles of ground glass. It is a very versatile material to use with glass as it will broaden your colour palette and give countless different effects for your beads. Each colour will stay separate so you can use this fact to your advantage.

Materials needed

- Red and pale green enamel powders
- Small metal reservoir
- Prepared mandrel and bead release
- Rod in ivory glass
- Enamel sieve

Designer Tip

Make a note of the coloured enamels used for each bead you make so you can always reproduce the colours if you need to.

Place an enamel powder in a suitable metallic container. Make an ivory bead, allow it to firm up and then reheat the surface. Roll the bead in the powder **A**, moving it around in the container to cover the surface area of the glass.

As the bead cools, bring back into the heat and melt the enamel onto the surface in the flame. Repeat until you have an even red glossy surface **B**.

The bead can now be decorated. Add additional enamel colouring by sprinkling the powder with a special enamel sieve **C**. Apply heat to secure the enamel to the glass . Either melt it in flush, or leave as a textured coating.

Technique Tips

CoE rules apply to enamels so use the correct enamels for the type of glass that you are using.

Always use an extraction system when working with enamels plus a nose and mouth mask. Do not inhale the fine glass particles from enamels into your lungs.

Enamelled stringer

Another use for enamel is to melt it into the glass before pulling as a stringer to create a range of decorative stringers. Pale colours are often used as base colours.

Materials needed

- Thick rod in transparent pale turquoise
- White enamel
- Flat-nosed tweezers

Select the turquoise glass rod and melt a large gather at the tip. Roll the hot glass into the mound of white enamel 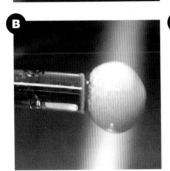.

Take the rod and gather to the flame and melt the enamel onto the surface. Repeat several times until the enamel is well mixed into the gather 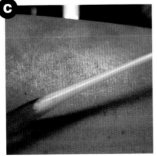.

Pull the gather slowly to make a thick stringer, or pull it more quickly to make a thinner stringer 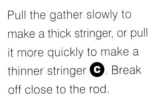. Break off close to the rod.

Boiled enamel beads

This is one of the simplest beads to make and has great results. Using different-coloured enamels can look stunning.

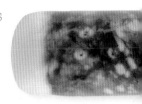

Materials needed

- Teaspoon each of red, pale green and black enamels
- Marver
- Prepared mandrel and bead release
- Rod in ivory glass

Place the enamel powders on the marver. Make a cylinder base bead from light ivory. Roll the bead onto each of the powders in turn 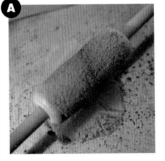, melting them in.

Put the bead in the flame and heat the surface just away from the tip of the torch. Both the glass and the enamel will begin to boil. Heat until the surface area has boiled and created a mottled effect .

Due to the high temperatures you may need to reshape the bead . Place in a kiln to anneal in the normal manner.

ENCASED BEADS

There are several methods of encasing beads, which may depend on the type of bead you are making. The gather method is suitable for a small bead and can produce a thick layer of glass, while winding is suitable for a long bead.

Glass gather

Materials needed

- Rod of clear glass
- Flat-nosed tweezers
- Small donut bead (prepared)
- Pusher tool (or small masher)

When working with any transparent glass, especially clear, it is vital to remove any debris or scumming (air bubbles) from your rod before you start. Melt the top of your rod and with a pair of tweezers remove the tip slowly, breaking it off in the flame without creating a trail **A**, which will in turn create unwanted air bubbles. Discard the unwanted glass and continue to use your clean rod.

Your base bead must remain firm (but warm) at all times whilst the clear glass is being added. Hold your bead below the flame and slightly to the side. With a clean transparent rod melt a large gather **B** at least double the size of your base bead.

Heat the gather slowly and carefully in the 'melting' area of the flame, taking care not to boil or contaminate the

glass with scum. The gather needs to be at the molten stage before you lower it down onto the glass and, in one continuous movement, encase the central area **C** of your bead.

Wrap the glass once around the bead, then continue with the remains of the gather around one end of your bead (either to the left or the right). Build up the side to create a lip of clear glass that will eventually be melted around the mandrel **D**. Melt the rod off from your bead carefully, once again to avoid air bubbles.

The bead will now have one exposed end. Gently heat the area where the encasing glass overlaps and, with a pair of flat-nosed tweezers, push the excess into the small 'V' shape that was formed. Reheat the tip of your rod to a molten state and fill in, and complete the second end with a lip **E** as for the previous end.

Return the bead to the flame and begin to soften the glass, forming lips at the ends. With a pusher tool (or small masher), help the lip of glass cover the ends towards the mandrel, without touching the mandrel with the glass. Continue heating the bead until the encasing layer has fully melted and covered **F** your base bead. Anneal in a kiln in the usual manner.

Wound glass

This method relies on a continuous supply of molten glass from the encasing rod, using a spiral action around the bead.

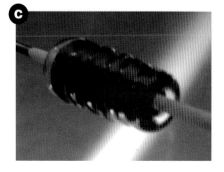

Materials needed

- Cylinder bead (prepared)
- Rod in clear glass
- Marver
- Pusher tool (or small masher)

Melt the tip of the rod, holding the base bead below the flame. Wrap the encasing glass around the bead in a spiral action, holding the rod in the melting area of the flame **A**. The glass is applied with a slight pressure. The layers of the spiral wrap also need to overlap to eliminate air bubbles.

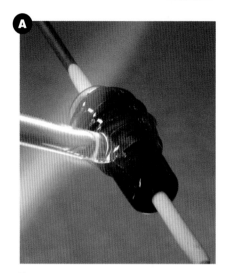

When you reach the end of the bead, continue on to make a lip. Return to the beginning of the spiral wrap, reheat and push the excess glass into the 'V' shape **B**. Add more glass to create a second lip.

Start to melt the encasing layer **C**, using a marver to smooth and straighten both the sides and ends. Use a pusher tool (or small masher) to push the lip over the edge of the bead. Anneal in a kiln in the normal manner.

Encased shapes

This fairly simple technique is a good way to practise your encasing skills. These beads incorporate manipulation of dots to achieve triangles and stripes. Use clear glass or pale transparent colours to encase your beads.

Triangles

Materials needed

- Prepared mandrel and bead release
- Rods in two transparent blues, white and clear glass
- Flat-nosed tweezers

Make a small donut base bead in blue before applying four white dots at each end of the bead. Alternate the second set of dots in the spaces created by the first set **A**. Make the dots small. When they are melted they should remain as circles and not become distorted.

When the bead has firmed up, cover the eight white dots with a lighter transparent blue colour **B**. Heat only

the tip of the glass rod and then press down firmly, trying to cover the white dot completely. Using more than one transparent colour will add extra effect to your bead.

Using an even, 'all over' heat, melt the dots flush to the surface of the bead. With the additional glass, the dots become enlarged and distort into triangular shapes **C**. You could finish

your bead here without encasing it, either by leaving it plain or decorating it with raised dots.

To further enhance the triangles and to encase your bead, wrap two or three rings of clear or light transparent glass around the centre of the bead **D**. Each additional wrap of glass will increase the size of your bead and the magnification of the triangles.

Melt the encasing layer by directing the flame on to the top of the ring **E**. Use flat-nosed tweezers (or mashers) to keep the encasing ring straight whilst heating. Hold your mandrel parallel at all times during this stage or your ring will quickly become 'off centre' and your triangles will become distorted.

Let your bead firm up in the normal manner **F**. Stack several layers of white and coloured dots to produce a more detailed triangular effect.

Stripes

The result of this technique will be an encased striped bead, using a base bead and two colours.

Materials needed

- Prepared mandrel and bead release
- Rod in base colour
- Rods of black and white
- Rod of clear or light glass
- Marver

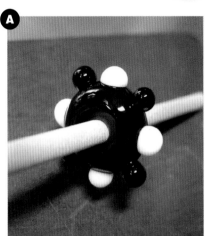

Start by making a fairly narrow donut bead in a base colour. Place two sets of four alternating dots in contrasting colours. Flash-heat each dot as you apply to 'round off' in shape and to 'fix' the dot **A** to the base bead.

Using an encasing rod of clear or light transparent glass, wrap two or three rings of glass around the centre of the bead. On the second and subsequent wraps, apply slight pressure to the rod using a marver to widen the encasement ring towards the outside edges **B** of your bead.

Apply heat to the encasing ring to 'round off' your bead **C**. Anneal in the kiln in the usual manner.

MILLEFIORI

The word *millefiori* means 'a thousand flowers' in Italian. Most millefiori comes from the island of Murano in Venice and has distinctive decorative patterns. An advanced lampworker can make their own millefiori, but most choose to buy commercial millefiori.

Materials needed

- Millefiori slices
- Marver
- Rod of black glass
- Rod of clear glass
- Flat-nosed tweezers
- Prepared mandrel and bead release

Millefiori is a cane (called a murrine) with coloured patterns, which can only be seen from the cut ends of the cane. The murrine is heated in a furnace, and 'pulled' until narrow, while still maintaining its interior design. When cooled it is cut to provide a range of colourful slices of glass to use for decoration. Lay your selection of Millefiori slices on a marver and select four slices of Millefiori glass **A**.

Using flat-nosed tweezers (or mashers) choose and pick up a selection of glass that has the same thickness and a level surface. Make a black base bead and allow it to firm up. Bring back to the flame, heat the area required for your first millefiori slice until it is glowing red. Using flat-nosed tweezers (or mashers) pick up a slice of millefiori and place it with a little pressure onto your bead **B** to secure.

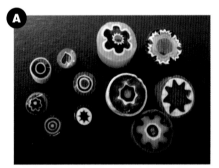

Technique Tip

Millefiori from Murano has a CoE of 104, so it is important to check compatibility with your glass before you purchase. All millefiori is compatible with Moretti rods and Moretti glass.

Repeat the positioning until you have four slices on your bead **C**. Keeping all the slices warm whilst you work, carefully cover the tops of the slices with a small dot of clear glass. This will stop the patterns becoming distorted as you complete the encasing.

With a clear rod, melt a large pea-size gather until it is molten and fluid. Place large dots in between the millefiori slices **D**, pushing down with your glass rod to force the glass into the crevices.

Continue adding clear glass onto the two sides of the bead, making sure that your millefiori slices are completely encased **E**. Air bubbles will be trapped in the edges of your glass slice unless your encasing glass is very hot and flows into the 'corners' of your bead.

When sufficient encasing glass has been added, take it back to the flame and melt the encasing layer. Direct the flame at the centre of the bead **F** and then to each of the ends. Use a pair of flat-nosed tweezers (or mashers) to straighten the glass if necessary.

Anneal the bead in a kiln when it is complete. This 'cold' bead shows the millefiori slices in their true colours against a background of black **G**. This simple millefiori bead has just four slices, but any number or placement pattern can be used with the same technique.

Designer Tip

Handcrafted by the finest Murano glassmakers, millefiori adds an exciting flair to any project.

E

F

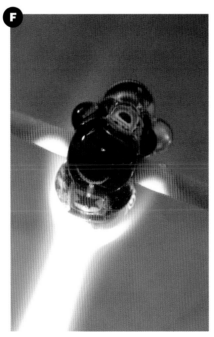

G

FOIL BEADS

Gold and silver leaf is sold in little booklets with a thin layer of tissue paper separating the sheets. It is very difficult to handle as the leaf will stick to almost anything and easily flies away. Gold and silver leaf is used to create beautiful decorative effects in lampwork beads. These techniques show how to apply both gold and silver leaf.

Gold leaf

Materials needed

- Foil leaf in gold
- Rod of black glass
- Tweezers
- Marver
- Prepared mandrel and bead release

To cut the gold leaf, keep the leaf sandwiched between the layers of tissue paper, and cut into random shapes. Use tweezers to separate the tissue from the leaf and place the leaf onto a marver ready for use **A**.

Make a black bead and allow it to cool slightly and firm up, but at the same time keeping the bead warm in the tip of the flame. Pick up a small piece of leaf with your pair of tweezers, bring your bead out of the flame and position the leaf onto your bead **B**. Using the tweezers, press the edges of the leaf in contact with the glass. Keep the bead warm at all times by returning it to the tip of the flame.

Add more leaf to the bead and marver the bead to secure the leaf in close contact with the glass **C**. Pay special attention to secure the leaf at the ends of the bead. Complete adding the leaf and fully marver your bead before putting back into the flame.

Bring the bead back into the flame **D** to fire polish. Any leaf not secured to the glass will now burn away. Take care not to overheat the bead at this stage. Anneal in the kiln in the usual manner.

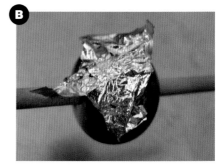

Silver leaf

You can completely encase a bead in silver leaf for a different effect. Encasing the bead in clear glass is an option for both silver and gold foil.

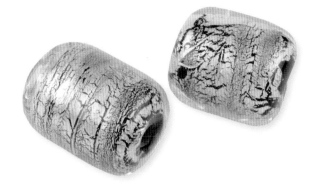

Materials needed

- Prepared mandrel and bead release
- Foil leaf in silver
- Rod of base colour
- Marver
- Rod of clear glass

Cut a strip of silver leaf long enough to wrap around your bead **A** several times and cover the ends. Place the leaf on a marver and prepare a cylinder bead. Allow to firm up and then reheat the surface to a warm glow and roll the bead over the silver leaf.

The leaf will easily attach itself to the bead. Roll the bead back and forth to secure the leaf, including the foil at each end **B** of the bead.

Keeping the bead warm, but out of direct contact with the flame, encase your silver bead in clear glass using the winding encasing method **C**.
If the silver gets too hot at any time, the leaf will break down and disappear with the heat.

The silver bead **D** may now be finished in the usual manner in a kiln or used as the core to create a more intricately decorated bead.

EMBEDDING ZIRCONIA

Zirconia are loose faceted gemstones that have the look and sparkle of diamonds, which makes them popular in making jewellery. There is a huge variety of colours, cuts and shapes. Embedding a bead with floral zirconia gemstones is undertaken using several layers of glass.

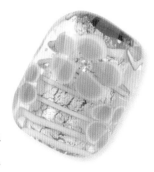

Materials needed

- Prepared mandrel and bead release
- Rod of blue transparent glass
- Silver leaf
- Marver
- Encased green stringer or filigrano rod
- Rod of white glass
- Rods of light and dark shades of purple glass
- Tweezers
- Four clear ¹⁄₁₆in (2mm) Zirconia gemstones
- Rod of clear glass
- Shaping tool
- Sharp-pointed tool

Make a slim blue cylinder bead and apply a layer of silver leaf A. Marver and reheat the bead in the cooler part of the flame to avoid burning off the silver.

Using an encased green stringer or filigrano rod, apply a thin layer to the bead using the spiral wrapping technique B. There is no need to encase the ends of your bead as yet.

Start to make the flowers by laying down four sets of five dots in an evenly spaced pattern C to make up the petals of a flower. The flowers can be made with any number of dots according to the design you require. White is normally used as the base colour for the petals, but other opaque colours can also be used. The centre of each group of petals will be the site for the zirconia.

Technique Tip

You must remember to keep the whole bead warm when dropping in zirconia. However, this needs to be done with care and without rotating the mandrel as you drop in the gemstones.

Melt the white base dots flush with the bead and apply transparent coloured dots in the centre of each to give your flower a coloured petal **D**. Again, melt flush. To give additional depth and graduation of colour, apply a second, darker-coloured transparent dot on each petal, towards the centre of the flower.

To add a zirconia stone to the centre of each flower, apply heat to a cluster of petals until it glows red. Take out of the flame, wait until the colour just re-appears and with a sharp pointed tool, make an indentation in the centre **E**.

Lay out the stones so that they are all facing with the flat side facing upwards. With a pair of tweezers, pick up a zirconia stone. Flash-heat the flower where you are going to place the stone, bring out of the flame and very carefully drop the zirconia into the centre cavity. Take back to the flame and flash-heat the flower **F** again to 'seat' the stone into the bead. If you did not place the zirconia stones this would simply create a small air bubble at the centre of each flower.

The bead is then encased for a second time using clear glass. The usual rules apply in obtaining an even casing, which is extended over the ends of the bead **G** to allow encasing up to the mandrel.

Apply heat to melt the encasing layer, working one end at a time to avoid distortion of the whole bead **H**. Marver the bead at regular intervals and avoid making the centre of the bead too hot.

Shape the ends **I** by pushing the layer of encasing glass towards the mandrel with a shaping tool. Finish off the bead by annealing in a kiln in the usual manner.

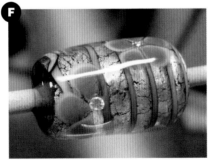

METALLIC EFFECTS

You can use metal directly in beadwork; use fine silver wire to create a raised globular texture around a bead or use silver mesh around or within a bead for decoration. Reduction glass (frit) also gives a metallic lustre to a bead.

Materials needed

- Prepared mandrel and bead release
- Rod of red glass
- 0.3mm (28 gauge) fine silver round wire
- Tweezers

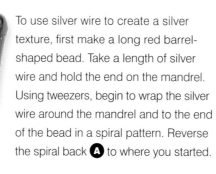

To use silver wire to create a silver texture, first make a long red barrel-shaped bead. Take a length of silver wire and hold the end on the mandrel. Using tweezers, begin to wrap the silver wire around the mandrel and to the end of the bead in a spiral pattern. Reverse the spiral back **A** to where you started.

When you have finished wrapping, burn off the wire **B** in the heat of the flame.

When heated, the wire dissolves into small globules, or silver balls **C**. There may also be a mark where the wire was first laid down. Burn off the wire at the edge of the mandrel to remove, if necessary, and anneal the bead in a kiln in the usual manner.

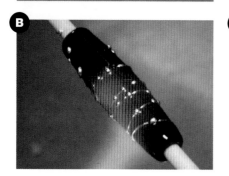

Silver mesh

This silver mesh is used within an encased bead. Added sparkle comes from using copper mica powder in the core bead.

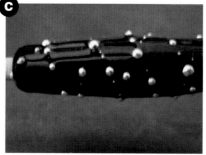

Materials needed

- Copper mica powder
- Marver
- Prepared mandrel and bead release
- Rod of dark amber glass
- Strip of silver mesh
- Rod of clear glass
- Tweezers
- Rod of light amber glass
- Pointed tool (or pick)

Spread mica powder on a marver. Make a small cylinder bead. Allow the bead to firm up before reheating the surface and roll in the mica powder. Marver the bead to secure the powder and encase in the amber glass **A**.

Heat the bead slowly and gently while encasing and shaping the bead to protect the mica from burning off.

Cut a strip of silver mesh and use a pair of tweezers to pick up the mesh and apply to the bead. Heat the bead, and also spot-heat a small area of clear glass until it is slightly fluid. Secure one end of the mesh to the hot area. Wrap the silver mesh around the bead in a spiral pattern **B**. Quickly marver the mesh to secure it to the bead.

Apply a second clear encasing layer, but do not overheat the inner core. Apply groups of three white and light amber dots, plunge the centre with a pick to produce flowers **C**. Reheat, shape and anneal.

Reduction glass

When worked in a propane-enriched flame, reduction glass will change the appearance of a bead to a beautiful metallic or iridescent sheen on the surface.

Materials needed

- Prepared mandrel and bead release
- Rod of pale bullseye glass
- Bullseye reduction lustre rod (CoE of 96)

Using a normal working flame, make a base bead in a pale colour and wrap with a reduction lustre rod **A**. Take the bead out of the flame and allow it to firm up until the glow of the bead has disappeared.

Increase the size of the flame by turning up the propane until the cones at the tip of the torch are approximately 1½–2in (4–5cm) long. Bring the bead back into the 'tip' of the flame for a few seconds **B**, making sure that all surfaces feel the effect.

As soon as the metallic finish appears **C**, place the bead in the kiln. If you introduce it back into a neutral flame, the metallic sheen will burn off and disappear. It is possible to try it again but the results are never as good.

SPECIAL TYPES OF GLASS

Making a bead with dichroic glass gives it an extra dimension and quality. Dichroic glass has a special coating on one side that both transmits and reflects light. Striking glass only establishes its full colour after it has been heated and cooled several times.

Dichroic glass

Materials needed

- Strip of copper foil
- Stamps
- Prepared mandrel and bead release
- Rod of dark green transparent glass
- Strip of clear-based green dichroic glass
- Tweezers
- Rods of clear glass
- Marver

Copper foil can be used with craft stamps to produce miniature cut-outs for use in glass beads. Smooth a piece of copper foil and use the stamps **A** to cut out shapes.

Make a thin cylinder bead with the dark green glass. Take a strip of green dichroic glass and hold it so that the special metallic coating is facing upwards. Hold the bead under the flame and, using tweezers **B**, bring the uncoated side of the dichroic glass into the flame. Wrap the strip around the bead.

The coated side of the dichroic glass **C** needs to be encased with clear glass, but you still need to be careful not to burn the dichroic coating in the flame. There is no need to encase the ends of the bead.

Using a gentle heat shape the bead back into a cylinder. Do not overheat the bead as it will still break down the coating on the dichroic glass. Add the copper foil by spot-heating **D** a small area where you want the first shape.

Pick up a copper shape with a pair of tweezers and place it on the bead. The colour of the copper will temporarily disappear with the heat and change to

a dark, ashen grey. Secure the copper shape firmly to the glass by pressing down with the tweezers and then rolling on the marver **E**. Repeat until you have completed the design.

Apply your second layer of clear glass, this time encasing the copper shapes and the ends of the bead **F**. Reheat, shape and finish off. Put into a kiln to anneal. The rich redness of the copper foil will return when your bead has finally cooled.

Technique Tip

Any bits of foil that do not adhere to the glass will tend to burn away in the heat.

Striking glass

Striking glass develops its true colour when it has been melted, cooled and then gently reheated for a second time.

Materials needed

- Prepared mandrel and bead release
- Rod of white glass
- Rods of striking glass in several colours

Make a white base bead. Wrap with a colour of striking glass. The bead will become pale transparent **A** in colour.

Allow the bead to cool until the glow has subsided. Do not adjust the flame but bring the bead back into the tip (cooler part) of the flame and wait for the colour **B** to gradually appear.

Bright yellow, red and ruby gold (Rubino Ora) are typical striking glass colours **C** to use. Rubino Ora is one of the most popular rods, producing a very deep pink colour when applied over a base of white.

Technique Tip

When buying striking rods, ask the supplier for detailed instructions on using them, as these may differ from the steps above depending on the rods you have purchased.

CHROMATIC IMPLOSION

In a chromatic implosion bead, you make a fine wheel, add implosion dots and melt them in before collapsing the wheel in on itself. It is an excellent way to work on your control of gravity as you melt the wheel along the mandrel itself. You can easily vary the shape of the bead by continuing to let the wheel run down the mandrel into a tube or 'cone', or shape back to an even bead.

Materials needed

- Thick prepared mandrel and bead release
- Rod in clear glass
- Stringer 1/16 in (2mm) in white glass
- Stringer 1/16 in (2mm) in pale blue glass
- Stringer 1/16 in (2mm) in medium blue glass
- Stringer 1/16 in (2mm) in dark blue glass

Using a thick mandrel and a rod of clear glass, begin to build a wheel with a fairly small bead (or footprint) **A**. The wheel is built up by keeping the mandrel horizontal and rotating at the same time.

Continue making your wheel, building up to as large a wheel as you feel comfortable with **B**, perhaps several inches wide.

Keep the wheel as round and uniform as possible. Use your white stringer and place five or six dots on one side of your wheel, placed closely around the mandrel **C**. Implosion beads tend to look better if the dots are placed on the left side.

Moving outwards, continue to place dots in a circle, first in pale and medium blue, then in dark blue **D**.

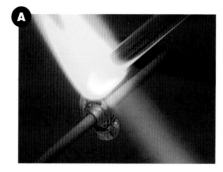

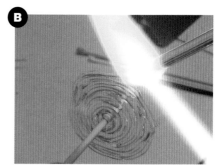

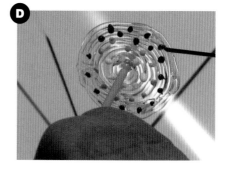

Always stay on one side of the wheel, and be sure to keep the whole wheel in the warmth of the flame.

Melt all the dots flat by quickly rotating the wheel with the dots facing the flame **E**. Keep the heat uniform. Do not let the wheel collapse at this point.

When you have melted the dots, start heating the edges of the wheel, so they begin to fold over the melted dots **F**. If you made your dots on the left side of the wheel, your bead should collapse to the left (and opposite if you created your beads on the right-hand side).

Keep the heat even, and go slowly. Continue to fold the bead over itself. Keep the heat uniform. Use gravity to your advantage **G**, but make sure the bead folds evenly, or you'll get a twisted implosion.

As the folded part of the wheel gets close to the mandrel, make sure it connects as evenly as possible **H**, to avoid creating sharp edges.

Shape and even out the bead again in the flame again, keeping it as level as possible, so your implosion **I** is crisp. You do not have to make a round bead; it may be a cone or cylinder shape. Finish off your bead in the kiln in the normal manner.

Technique Tips

Your finished bead will look better if you place the first ring of dots close to the mandrel.

The implosion will generally be more successful if you use plenty of dots.

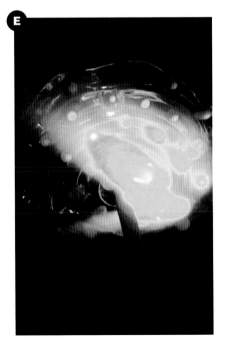

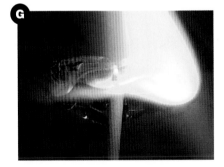

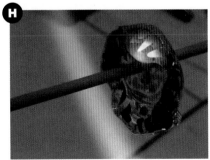

JEWELLERY AND TOOLS

Once you have made your lampwork beads you may want to use them to create ready-to-wear jewellery pieces. Commercial findings can be readily purchased online or from your favourite bead or craft store. To make your work truly unique, you can make your own findings using some basic tools and techniques.

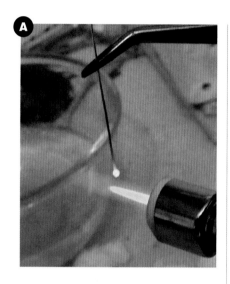

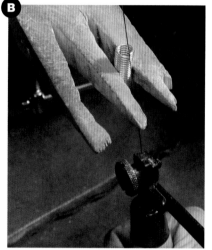

Headpins: To make a headpin, cut several lengths of ⅝in (0.6mm) Sterling silver or fine silver wire. Make them approximately 2in (5cm) long. Use tweezers with an insulated handle to hold one end of a piece of wire. Light a butane candy or jeweller's torch. Hold the wire so that the end is in the flame **A**. The end of the wire will melt and a small ball will form. Turn off the flame and quench the wire in cold water. Place the headpins in a pickle (acidic) solution to remove the fire scale, or sand and polish them.

Jumprings: You can easily make jumprings by wrapping wire around metal mandrels or similar items. Use dead soft or half-soft wire as it is easier to handle. Don't let your wire develop a slant as you wrap it, or else you will end up with oval-shaped jumprings. To make just a few jumprings, wind the wire tightly, keeping the wraps neatly and firmly close together. Make tight, even wraps by holding the wire under tension and pulling it as you wrap it **B**. Now, slide the coil off the mandrel and cut the rings with a jeweller's saw.

Split rings: Split rings are a secure method of connecting jewellery links together **C**. A split ring is made using the same method as a jumpring. When cutting the rings, cut the third loop so that you have one and a half wraps. Open the split ring with split-ring pliers.

Technique Tip

Use jumprings to make quick connections that bear only light weights on a piece of jewellery.

Basic pliers

Some of these basic pliers are required to make the jewellery and other items featured on the following project pages.

A Snipe/chain-nosed: These pliers have a very pointed tip on the jaws. They are used for making chain-links, for connecting findings and for wire wrapping.

B Crimping: Used to flatten a crimp to secure a strand of beads to a clasp. The crimp bead is fed into the back of the pliers' jaw and squashed flat. It is then held vertically and rounded off in the front groove of the jaws.

C Split ring: The hooked jaw of the pliers will separate the coil of a split ring, allowing you to slip on a jumpring or connecting finding.

D Bent-nosed: These pliers have a small, bent tip that sits on an angle to the jaws of the smooth-surfaced pliers. This allows you to get into difficult positions when working with wire or metal findings, or opening split rings.

E Round-nosed: These pliers are used mainly for creating loops at the end of necklaces, bracelets and earrings that connect to the fastening clasp. Both jaws on the pliers are round and taper towards the end.

F Flat-nosed: The flat jaw of these pliers will assist when making wire spirals, for opening and closing jumprings and for wire. They can have a blunt or pointed end. The pointed end is useful for when you are wrapping loops.

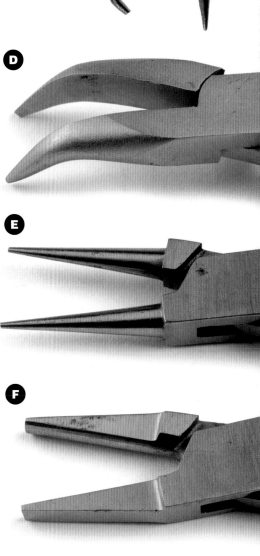

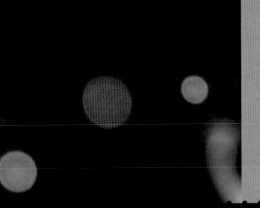

THE PROJECTS

create jewellery and home decor items

The projects in this section are contributed by lampworking artists. The projects are both functional and beautiful, making a range of items that are both practical and decorative. Each artist brings their own skills and influences to this section and shares their experience of how to successfully complete their designs. Once you have experienced some of the methods and techniques in this book, you should feel confident about attempting some of the projects and creating your own beautiful glasswork and jewellery.

Grecian Vessel Pendant

Use your flame-working skills to meld together history and molten glass into a softly curving modern-day artefact. Elaine Alhadeff shows you how to make a Greek amphora vessel to wear as a pendant. You can experiment with using opaque or transparent glass, adding surface texture or decoration, metals, frits or enamels to create a delicate old-world effect. For your first vessel, it is best to start small.

Materials and tools

For the vessel:

Rods of clear glass (for stringers)

Reduction frit in iris gold (small or medium)

Rods of transparent cobalt blue Effetre glass

Large prepared mandrel and bead release

Marver/marvering tools

Tweezers

For the stopper:

Tiny cork

½in–2in (1–5cm) long headpin

Round-nosed and chain-nosed pliers

Glass or gemstone bead

Sterling silver bead cap

2in (5cm) very fine silver chain

⅛in–¼in (3–6mm) jumprings

Tiny charm, crystal or gemstone

Wire cutters

For the chain:

20in–24in (50–60cm) of Sterling silver chain

Small crystals and silver beads

Clasp

1 Melt a small gather of glass on a clear rod and coat the gather with the gold reduction frit. Melt in the frit and dip again. Continue this until you have four to five layers of frit. Melt the frit in until smooth and pull into stringers about ½in (1cm) thick. Set the stringers aside for later.

Technique Tip

It's easy to get caught up in technique, so remember to continually flash your bead in the flame to keep all parts warm while you work.

2 Wind on a small bead using the blue glass. This should be placed approximately ¾in–1in (2–2.5cm) from the end of the mandrel. The distance between the bead and the end of the mandrel will determine the size of your vessel. Heat and centre the bead.

3 Gently marver the bead into a small cylinder. Using a marvering tool, clean up the ends so they are straight. The cylinder should be well centred and at least ¼in (6mm) in length. Add more glass if needed to reach the approximate size. This forms the neck of the vessel.

4 Wind a ½in (1cm) disk onto the end of the mandrel and another onto the lowest end of the neck. Be sure to keep both ends warm by continuously rotating the mandrel back and forth through the flame as you work. These discs form the shoulder and base of the vessel.

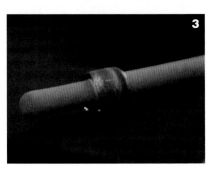

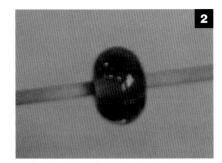

Technique Tip

Be sure to check carefully for holes when you have finished coiling the glass. They appear as a bright spot or an area that is sinking.

5 Begin adding coils of glass onto each disc alternately, each coil being placed slightly to the inside of the last. Keep in mind an egg shape. You should have two small cups facing each other, with the end cup slightly smaller in diameter. Keep all parts warm as you work.

6 Continue adding coils until the two sides touch. Wind some glass onto the end. Spot-heat one area and use the tip of your tweezers to coax the two sides together. Continue around, heating and sealing. Gently warm the entire piece, sealing up any lingering holes, which are critical to the structure of your piece.

7 Start heating the glass very gently. It will start to smooth out and puff up. Once this happens, begin to gently marver it into shape. Be careful not to get the glass too hot at any time. You will need plenty of patience here as you heat in the flame and then marver repeatedly until you reach the required shape that will form the basis of the vessel.

8 Next add a small lip to the neck. Make a pea-sized gather and lightly attach it to the top edge of the neck, keeping the thickness uniform as you wrap. Heat gently in to seal and smooth, then marver to shape and even it out.

9 For the handles, place two small dots as markers for their positioning, one at the shoulder and another 1/4in (5–7mm) below for the lower connection. Repeat this on the other side of the vessel. Heat a pea-sized gather, attach to the top dot, pull away and wait a few seconds for the glass to cool. Curve the glass down and connect to the lower dot. Spot-heat each area where the handles attach to the dots, making sure they are well sealed onto the surface. Using a cylinder tool and the tweezers, curve, shape and sculpt the handles until you are satisfied with how they look. Be sure to keep the entire piece warm as you work.

Designer Tip

To attach the vessel onto a neckpiece, string tiny seed-bead or gemstone loops through the handles, or a beaded collar around the neck.

10 Using the gold stringer, start to create a dot pattern of your choice on the surface of the vessel.

11 Evenly heat the dots to uniform size, leaving them raised. Gently heat the piece all over, place in a reduction flame (i.e. turn up the propane or reduce the oxygen slightly) until the dots reduce. Place the glass in a kiln. The final step to take is to make the stopper for the amphorae.

12 Poke a hole down the centre of a tiny cork and push a headpin up through it. Using pliers to help, place a co-ordinating bead on top and add a bead cap. Before you wire wrap the headpin, connect some chain between the top and handle, then add a dangle from the loop and a jumpring. Use wire cutters to cut and trim. Attach a neck chain to the handles with jump rings, decorated with crystals and beads. Finish off with a clasp of your choice.

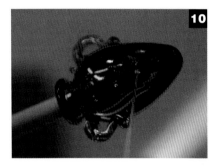

Bead Earrings

Make these beautiful organic lentil beads created by Emma Baird and turn them into a unique piece of jewellery using fine pure silver leaf and mesh.

Materials and tools

For the beads:

Rod of ivory glass

Prepared mandrel and bead release

Lentil-press

Paddle marver

Fine silver leaf

Rod of intense black glass (prepared as stringer)

Tweezers

Fine silver mesh

For the earrings:

4 x ⁵⁄₃₂in (4mm) crystal beads

2 x Sterling silver headpins

Round-nosed pliers

2 x Sterling silver earrings

Flat-nosed pliers

Flush-cutters

1 Warm the rod of ivory glass in the flame. Begin to wind the glass onto the mandrel and check it against the cup of the lentil-press regularly. Continue until your footprint is about ¹⁄₂₁in (1mm) short of each edge.

2 Continue to wind glass onto the mandrel until you have a melon shape. Roll the bead into the silver leaf on a marver and burnish it onto the bead to prevent it from 'burning off' in the flame. Return to the flame and apply a good deal of heat to allow the glass to react with the silver. Let the glass swirl to create a lovely pattern.

Designer tip

Make several beads to ensure you have a pair that match in size and shape for your earrings.

3 Keeping the glass hot and soupy, take the black stinger and drizzle the glass onto the bead. You don't need to apply very much of this glass; just a little applied over the bead will be enough. Heat the bead again and allow the glass to react with the heat.

4 Heat the bead until it is an even shape. Remove it from the flame and keep rotating the bead as it firms up a little. Keep rotating as you place it in the lentil-press. Align the top part of the press and gently push the top down onto the bead. Return to the flame.

5 Have silver mesh ready on the marver. Spot-heat the area where you want to place your mesh; it needs to be really hot to pick up the silver. Press the heated part of the bead into the mesh and burnish it on to make sure every part is in contact with the bead. Place back into the flame and heat the mesh. Press the bead again if need be and flame polish. Anneal in the kiln.

6 For the earrings, thread a crystal bead, lampwork bead and another crystal onto a headpin. Grip the silver wire of the headpin with the round-nosed pliers and push the wire away from you. Rotate the pliers away from you, and wrap the wire around the pliers in a loop. Attach an earring, grip the loop with the pliers and the wire with flat-nosed pliers. Pull the wire around the headpin creating a wrap. Trim off the excess wire with the flush-cutters. Repeat to make a pair.

Technique Tips

At the start, lay out some silver leaf on your marver. Cut a small amount of silver mesh and lay this next to your marver so it is ready to use.

Pull the black rod into a stringer before you start: heat the rod until you have a ball of molten glass at the end of the rod, then remove from the flame. Grab with tweezers and pull into a stringer.

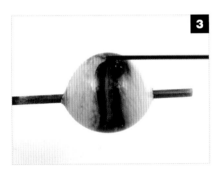

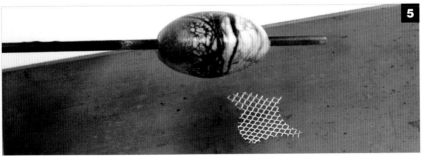

Bead Ring

This creation by Emma Baird sets a beautiful lampwork bead on a pure silver ring. It is a piece of jewellery that makes a real statement. By using a stainless steel nut and bolt to hold the bead, the need to fire the bead in place is removed. This ensures that the bead doesn't 'fume', so keeping its vibrant colours. Choose a bead for a ring that will create a piece of jewellery that is unique to you.

Materials and tools

For the bead:

Prepared mandrels and bead release

One glass rod of opaque dark turquoise and EDP Effetre glass

Marver

For the ring:

Ring sizing gauge and paper

Ring mandrel

1oz (25g) Art Clay Silver 650

Work mat and texture sheet

Release agent (olive oil or badger balm)

4 playing cards

Spacers of 1/32in (1mm) and 1.5 mm (1/16in)

Triangle and round cutter

Clay roller

Tissue blade cutter

Heat gun

Art Clay Silver syringe

Sanding pads and rubber block

Round needle file and large metal file

Stainless steel bolt and screw

Brass brush and polishing cloth

Bicarbonate of soda and liver of sulphur

Bead reamer

Lampwork bead

Anvil

2-part epoxy

1 Make a base bead with the dark turquoise glass. Make sure it is even and allow it to cool as you begin to warm the tip of a rod of EDP (Evil Devitrifying Purple). Once the rod is warm, shape the end of it into a point on your marver. Add four dots around the centre of the bead and four more in between them. Add eight dots evenly on each side of the centre dots.

2 Now melt the dots flat, but try and prevent them from distorting. If the bead itself gets too hot, then the dots will move and the pattern will be spoiled. Keep the bead below the flame and only heat the dots. Once melted, briefly heat the entire bead to reshape. Keep the bead warm as you prepare for the next step.

1

3 Take the dark turquoise rod of glass and warm the tip in the flame. Shape the tip into a point on your marver. Keeping the bead warm but firm, add small dots to the central purple dots and then to the ones on each side. Slowly melt the dots flat. If the EDP has turned matt, give the entire bead a flame bath until the gorgeous purple colour reappears. Anneal the bead in a kiln.

4 Using a Japanese ring sizing gauge, measure your chosen finger. You need to make your ring three sizes larger to allow for shrinkage. Place the sized-up ring gauge on the mandrel and mark with a pencil on either side of it, then mark clearly in the centre of your two lines. Now wrap a ring sizing paper around the mandrel, lining up the dark line on the non-sticky side with your pencil mark.

5 Place the clay in cling film and massage to make it soft. Prepare your work mat and texture sheet with release agent. Place two playing cards under each of the $1/32$in (1mm) spacers. Roll out the clay. Replace the cards with $1/32$in (1mm) spacers and clay on top of your texture mat. Use a triangular cutter to cut, then drape the shape over a bead slightly larger than the one you will set on your bead. Make a pilot hole in the centre and allow the clay to dry. Repeat the step to make a circle, but do not place over the bead and leave to dry. Now place two playing cards under each of the $1/16$in (1.5mm) spacers.

2

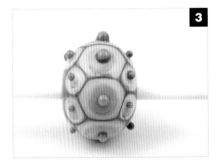

3

4

5

6 Roll out the clay into a long slab. Remove the cards and place the clay in between the 1/16in (1.5mm) spacers on top of your chosen texture and roll. Do this only once to ensure a clean impression of the texture on the clay.

7 Trim the clay so the sides are even. Moisten the ring sizing paper with a damp finger and drape the clay on the mandrel, following the paper's guideline. Allow the clay to overlap itself. Cut through the overlapping clay on the diagonal with a tissue blade cutter. Use the syringe to attach the ends of the seam together. Slide the ring on the mandrel and dry with a heat gun. Remove the ring from the mandrel, remove the paper, reinforce the seam inside and out with the syringe and dry thoroughly.

8 Once dry, refine your ring, disc and triangle using sanding pads and a rubber block. Handle with care. Use a round needle file to file out the centre of the disc until the stainless steel screw will sit snugly in the hole. Extrude some syringe into the hole before placing the screw into it. Reinforce a little with more syringe to ensure the screw is entirely embedded. Dry.

9 To make a strong ring the disc with the screw will be attached to the area where the seam is. Using a file, file this area of the ring to flatten it a little. File the bottom of the disc to ensure this is also flat and will fit nicely on the ring. Use a generous amount of syringe on the top of the ring shank and attach the disc with the screw and ensure they are securely attached. Dry.

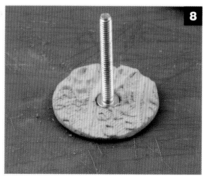

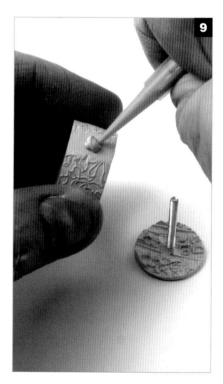

10 Push the bolt into a small ball of clay. Remove the bolt and the clay that has filled the centre of the bolt. Return the bolt to the clay and dry. Sand down to a shape and size in keeping with your bead. Check all pieces are dry and refined and fire in a kiln, supporting the shaped triangle in either vermiculite or fibre blanket.

11 Once the silver is fired and cool, brush with a brass brush. Tumble or hand polish with polishing papers for a high shine. To give it a patina, wash in a paste of bicarbonate of soda and water, and immerse in water with a couple of drops of liver of sulphur. Buff up with a polishing cloth to give the raised parts of the texture a shine.

12 Ream out your bead with a bead reamer until it fits the screw. Assemble the triangle and the bead on the post and place on an anvil. Take a metal file and file the post down. Remove any burrs by filing around the top of the bolt. Regularly check the bolt until it fits. When it does, apply a little two-part epoxy to the top of the screw and attach the bolt. Allow the glue to dry.

Technique Tip

Wherever possible, fire the rings from cold in the kiln. Fire at 1472°F (800°C) for a minimum of 30 minutes for a strong ring.

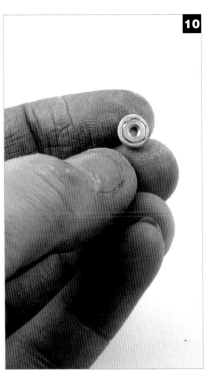

Encased Bead Bracelet

Create this beautiful bracelet by Beverley Hicklin using simple lampwork and silverwork techniques. The stunning beads combine encased layers of transparent colour with twisted stringer detail and handmade murrini. Varying the size and shape of your beads allows you the freedom to experiment and create a number of items. A large version would make a stunning focal bead while miniature versions are perfect for creating earrings.

Materials and tools

For the beads:

Prepared mandrels and bead release

Rods of clear glass

Rods of glass in shades of purple, green and aqua

Rod of silvered glass

Two different twisted stringers

Lentil-press (optional)

Murrini chips

Hooks:

¹⁄₁₆in (2mm) Sterling or fine round silver wire

Round-nosed pliers

Ball pein or chasing hammer

Bead caps:

¹⁄₆₄in (0.5mm) Sterling silver sheet and disk cutter

Round Sterling silver disks (to size)

Patterned metal stamps

Hammer

Doming block and punches (optional)

1 Start with the clear rods and apply random daubs of glass to the mandrel. Continue to make wraps of glass in purple and green. The larger you want the finished bead, the larger you should make this initial bead. Melt in the wraps to make smooth.

2 Take a twisted stringer (twistie) – this one is made from transparent aqua and silvered glass – and make a continuous wrap around the bead.

3 Melt in your twistie into the bead until it is smooth. To 'activate' the silver colour in the silvered glass twistie, use a reduction flame (i.e. turn up the propane or reduce the oxygen slightly) to create the effect.

4 Now encase your bead with clear glass. This is optional, but by encasing it you create a layered effect, which gives your finished bead more depth and interest.

Technique Tips

Experiment with a combination of transparent and opaque colours to achieve different effects.

Try making a variety of twisted stringers in different styles and colourways and vary the position to show movement and variety.

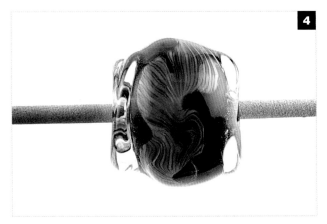

5 To do the encasing, start at the left hole and apply a thin layer of glass, working across to the right. Here you can see where the glass has been extended out over the right hole in a tube shape.

6 Turn the bead to face the flame and slowly heat the extension tube. The glass will draw towards the heat, so when you heat the tube it will melt down to completely encase your bead. Repeat on the left if necessary. You can now shape the bead – a lentil-press can be used for this.

7 Using another twistie – this time made from clear and white glass – repeat the wrap around the bead. Vary the positioning of the twistie so you don't follow the one you placed earlier.

8 Melt in and reshape the glass, if necessary. The final touch is to add some chips of murrini – these ones are made from clear and white glass. Gently heat the murrini and press down using a marver. Repeat the bead a number of times and at different sizes for the bracelet, and put into a kiln to anneal.

9 Make a hook clasp for the bracelet using the round fine silver wire. Measure off 3⅛in (8cm) and using round-nosed pliers, bend into shape. Using a ball pein or chasing hammer and working on a hard surface, repeatedly strike the hook to create a hammered finish.

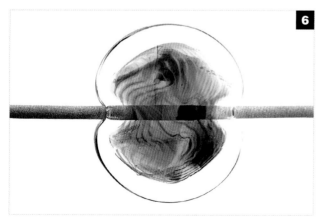

10 To create the bead caps, use a disc cutter to cut the silver sheet. (If you don't have a disk cutter, you can skip this step and buy some pre-punched discs from jewellery suppliers.) Carefully cut your discs to the appropriate size for the beads you are using – these ones measure 7/16in (12mm) in diameter.

11 Drill or punch a hole in the centre of the disk and then stamp a pattern on one side using a metal stamp. Working on a hard surface, strike the stamp firmly with a household hammer, but hit the stamp only once in the correct position or you'll create a ghost image. Repeat to cover the surface.

12 Once your disc has been patterned you will need to make the discs into a dome shape to fit your beads. One method is to use a brass doming block with a doming punch. Place the discs in the appropriate-sized hole and shape the discs by striking the punch with a hammer. Assemble to complete the bracelet.

Designer Tip

When using metal and patterned stamps, try using letters to create words – practise on a scrap piece of copper or aluminium.

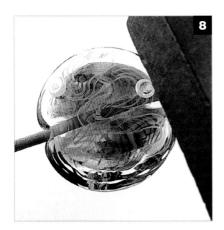

Champagne Bead Stopper

This simple, yet stunning bottle bead stopper by Beverley Hicklin creates a beautiful marbling effect in glass. The bead was created by building up layers of glass and colour before melting down into a round shape. It is simple to do but does require skill in controlling the glass as it melts. You can alter the thickness of each layer and so the final shape of your bead.

Designer Tip

Experiment with different colour combinations, such as simple black and white layers or twisted stringers.

Materials and tools

For the base bead:

Large prepared mandrel (2.4mm) and thick bead release

Rods in shades of turquoise, aqua, purple and green

Rod of silvered glass

Rod of clear glass

Marver (optional)

To complete:

Metal wine stopper

1 Start the bead by applying thin wraps of coloured glass to the mandrel. If you want to make a large bead, make your base fairly wide. Don't melt the bead smooth at this stage as you are going to build up layers of colour before melting in.

2 Continue to make wraps of glass in various colours. Try to build up the glass wraps evenly. Here the bead is about ¾in (2cm) wide, so glass has been applied across the width. Thinner layers make for a more interesting bead, but try not to apply the glass too perfectly.

3 Build up layers, using alternating colours. Don't have too many similar-toned colours next to each other. The effect is more interesting if you alternate tones and contrasts. Don't melt the bead yet.

4 You should not be put off by the shape of the bead at this stage. You will have a better pattern if you deliberately let various layers show through whilst you build up the bead. Try not to make the wraps too perfect.

5 Once you have built up plenty of different layers of colour, you can start to condense the disc down into a round shape. Gently and slowly heat the outer edge of the glass as you rotate the bead in the flame.

6 Rotating the bead in the heat can take a while, but don't rush this step. Too much heat too quickly could mean you lose control of the bead and end up with an unbalanced shape.

7 Once the glass has melted down and marbled patterns appear, reduce the flame, by increasing propane or reducing oxygen, to activate the colour of the silvered glass. Encasing the bead in clear glass will give depth to the piece.

8 To encase your bead in clear glass, start at the left hole and work across to the right. Extend the glass out over the right hole in a tube shape.

9 Turn the bead to face the flame and slowly heat the extension tube. The glass will be drawn towards the heat so if you have extended the tube out far enough, it will melt down to completely encase your bead at the hole. Repeat on the left to encase the hole if necessary. Finally, shape the bead using a marver, if required, and place in a kiln to anneal. The bead can then be threaded onto the wine stopper.

Technique Tips

This particular bead is quite large, but if you want smaller sizes, build your bead from a simple thin disk base.

Get interesting alternate effects by adding some frit in your layers by spinning the bead in your frit pot.

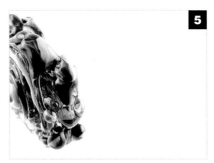

Squiggle Bead Necklace

These 'squiggle' beads with self-colour patterns are created by 'Jazzy Lily' (Pauline Holt). They are a celebration of colour, suitable for beginners. The necklace consists of knotting groups of glass and silver beads onto a silk thread. A central section is made up of glass drops and a star charm attached to a silver ring with oval jumprings. It is knotted to size, and silver and glass beads are tied to finish off the ends.

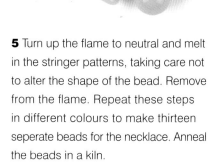

Materials and tools

For the beads:

Thin prepared mandrel and bead release

Coloured Bullseye rods (COE of 90)

Paddle marver

Rod in clear glass

Coloured stringers

For the necklace:

6 x glass drops/glass charms

Silver star charm

⅝in (15mm) silver ring

15 x small glass beads

7 x oval silver jumprings

Griffin silk bead cord no.10

30 x ¼in (6mm) round Sterling silver beads

2 x flat ¼in (6mm) silver beads

Scissors

1 Set your torch to a neutral flame. On a thin mandrel and using a coloured glass rod make a small tube (not too wide or thick) by rolling out a small bead onto a paddler marver. Remove any chill marks from the bead and keep it warm at the back of the flame.

2 Turn up the propane and create a gather at the end of a clear rod. The gather needs to be very hot, and wide enough to cover the bead.

3 Turn the clear rod vertically, then drop hot gather onto the bead, encasing the whole of the coloured tube. Turn the flame to neutral and shape the bead into a perfect round shape.

4 Allow the bead to cool a little and become solid – turn down the propane so the flame becomes narrow. Position the bead below and to the right of the flame. Using only the flame's warmth begin to make 'squiggles' around the bead.

5 Turn up the flame to neutral and melt in the stringer patterns, taking care not to alter the shape of the bead. Remove from the flame. Repeat these steps in different colours to make thirteen seperate beads for the necklace. Anneal the beads in a kiln.

6 To make the necklace, first attach the glass drops to the oval jumprings and the silver star charm to the silver ring. Arrange the squiggle beads and the small plain glass beads in two lines. This makes it easier when threading the main part of the necklace. Don't place the same two colours together.

7 Fully open the silk cord and at the very end of the thread make a double knot and thread on one silver and one small glass bead. Measure 6¼in (16cm) from the end of the thread and make a knot and thread on one silver, one small glass and a silver bead. Knot the thread next to the last bead. Measure 1¼in (3cm) from the last knot and make a knot, thread one silver, one small glass, one squiggle, one silver, one squiggle, one silver, one squiggle, one small glass and one silver bead. Knot close to the last bead.

8 Measure 1¼in (3cm) from the last knot. Thread one flat silver, one small round, one squiggle and one flat silver bead. Place the thread through the large silver ring with your charms already attached. Now thread back through the flat silver, the squiggle, the small round and the first flat bead. Adjust the thread and secure. Work on the other side of the necklace and repeat steps above to match.

When the last silver bead has been threaded, measure 6½in (170mm) and thread on one small glass and one round silver bead, and knot with a double knot and cut the thread. Hold both ends of the necklace, ensuring that the beads are equally spaced. Make a knot to join both ends together. Secure the hanging ends with a little 'fray stop'. The necklace is now ready for you to wear.

Technique Tip

When encasing, never get the clear glass on the mandrel – only on the coloured base.

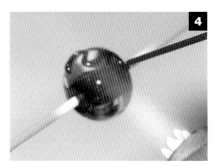

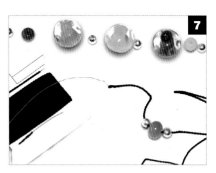

Catwalk Necklace

The necklace was created by 'Jazzy Lily' (Pauline Holt) and is a work of modern elegance; a piece of jewellery simply destined for the catwalk. It is a large sculptural bead created from borosilicate and dichrotic glass, which give it an exotic look and optical qualities. It has dramatic glass twists created around the bead, turning it into a unique necklace.

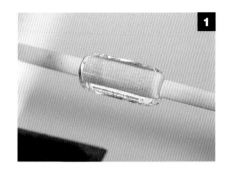

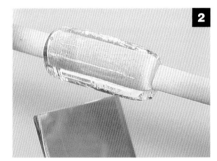

Materials and tools

Clear borosilicate glass rods

Thick mandrel, coated with bead release

Tweezers

CBS dichroic glass
1in (25mm) x ⅝in (16mm)

Paddle marver

1/32in (1mm) diameter
PVC tubing

4 large hole silver beads

1 Using a clear borosilicate rod and a thick mandrel, make a thin tube bead, no more than ⅔in (18mm) in length. Remove any chill marks and keep warm at the back of the flame.

2 Turn down the flame slightly and, using a pair of tweezers, pick up the strip of dichrotic glass. With the coated side facing away from you, warm the glass gently in the flame.

3 Heat a section on the bead gently and attach the strip of dichrotic glass. Use a graphite paddle to gently press the dichrotic strip around the bead. Where the two ends meet, take extra care to ensure that the join is well 'covered up'.

4 Turn up the flame and encase the whole bead in clear glass. As this is borosilicate glass it will take some time to work and you will need to use a very hot flame.

Technique Tip

You will need a high heat to work with borosilicate glass. Try a Nortel Minor Burner and an oxygen concentrator to reach the required temperatures.

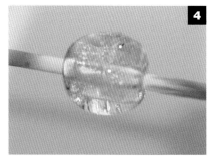

5 Once the bead is round and smooth, heat the end of a ¼–½in (6–7mm) glass rod. Keep the rod in the flame and then push the tip of the rod onto the centre of the bead. Twist the rod whilst at the same time pulling it gently away from the bead. When the twist is the desired height, burn off in the flame and smooth off any sharp points.

6 Place four twists around the centre of the bead and then four to the left and four to the right side. Check the position and angle of each twist. If any adjustments are needed, gently heat and use a marver to correct. To finish, thread onto plastic tubing and finish off with two handmade triangular Thai beads. Then the necklace just pops over the head without clasps and can be easily adjusted.

Grapevine Pendant

This necklace by Jan Jennings has been worked around a focal bead, created with a raised grapevine design with six co-ordinating glass spacers. The finished necklace has three graduating strands using glass seeds in gold tone, pearl and peacock blue, together with some vintage glass-faceted crystals, blue beads and Balinese silver beads.

Materials and tools

For hand-pulled stringers
1/32–1/16in (1–2mm):

Branches and leaves:

Rods of dark brown, raku, black, transparent mid-brown, pea green, transparent olive green glass

Grapes:

Rods of white, transparent violet blue, transparent amethyst glass

Uncoated mandrels for pulling stringers

For focal pendant:

Goldstone

Rods of crystal clear glass

Tweezers

Rod of ivory glass

Prepared mandrel and bead release

Mashers

Silvered ivory glass shards

Brass shaper

For the necklace:

Czech glass seeds in gold tone, pearl and peacock blue

Crystals, Balinese silver beads and six blue lampwork beads

1 Before making this focal bead you will need to have ready a number of hand-pulled stringers. These are pulled using uncoated mandrels (although other methods can be used). For the grapevine branches use brown, raku, black and mid-brown rods. For the leaves use a mix of pea green, raku, black and olive green rods. For the grapes use white encased with violet blue and amethyst rods, and violet blue on its own.

2 Goldstone stringers will also need to be pulled before starting your bead. Holding a pre-warmed piece of goldstone on the tip of a melted clear

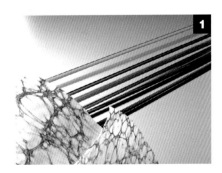

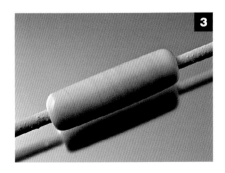

rod, fully encase the goldstone using a second clear rod. This is then fully heated and pulled into a stringer using a pair of tweezers.

3 With all the stringers and shards ready to hand, begin to make the cylinder bead starting with the desired size of footprint. The bead for this project is 1⅜in (34mm) hole to hole.

4 Continue to build the bead and shape as required. You can press the bead using mashers for a slim profile, but any shape you prefer can be used.

5 Working further out in the flame, where it is cooler, gently apply the shards. Spot-heat a small place on the bead and carefully touch the heated area with the edge of the shard. Gently apply heat pressing the shard using the brass shaper around the bead. Shards can be overlapped, left partially raised or melted smooth, depending on the finished look required.

6 Begin to apply the design using the pre-made stringers, working further out in the flame. If it is too hot it will cause the fine stringers to ball-up and become unworkable. Continue to build the design adding layers of dots for the grapes to create a three-dimensional effect. Keep the back of the bead warm throughout the whole decorating process to avoid cracking; it is very easy to get carried away with the decorating of the front and to forget about the rest of the bead, so work carefully. When complete, place the bead into a kiln for annealing.

7 The finished bead should be cleaned and ready to use for a necklace. The finished necklace is made as three graduating strands using Czech glass seed beads in gold tone, pearl and peacock blue, together with some vintage glass-faceted crystals and Balinese silver beads. Six lampwork beads are incorporated into the design of the main strand to complement the main focal bead. Attach the pendant firmly to the necklace and add a clasp at the back to complete the work.

7

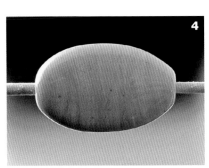

4

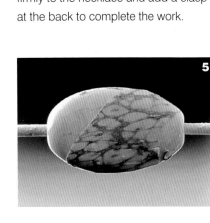

5

6

Organic Paperknife

This lampwork bead by Jan Jennings has been created with golden tones to co-ordinate with the gold tone of the paperknife. Neutral ivory, browns and sparkling goldstone are used with raised detail for added texture and interest. You will need to measure the length and diameter of your paperknife to determine the length of your bead and the size of mandrel you need to make it on.

Materials and tools

For the base bead:

Large mandrel and thick bead release

Glass rod in pale ivory

Raku frit (fine)

Goldstone ribbon

Marver

Glass rod in transparent light brown

Handmade twistie (prepared)

Silvered ivory glass shards

Tweezers

Brass shaper

Fine stringer (colours of your choice)

Aurae silver glass

To complete:

Golden-lustre glass spacer beads

Paperknife

Technique Tip

Before making the bead you will need to have ready a prepared twistie and a fine stringer colour of your choice for the raised decoration.

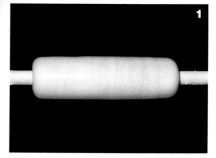

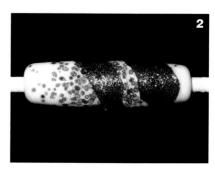

1 Begin by making the base bead in ivory to the length you require, keeping a slim cylinder shape. The finished bead is 1½in (38mm).

2 Add just a little raku frit and melt in smooth. Then add the goldstone ribbon. Gently melt this in smooth further out in the flame so as not to burn off the sparkles in the goldstone. Continue to heat and marver until your base is a pleasing shape and smooth. Next, whilst keeping the base warm, carefully encase the whole bead using light brown. Melt smooth and re-shape.

3 Apply the twistie in a random design. The twistie has been made by applying two or more colours of glass together and twisting the heated colours whilst gently pulling to create a thin rod of the twisted colours together. Melt smooth, keeping the shape of the bead in a long, cylinder form.

4 To apply shards (very thin pieces of blown glass), work further out in the flame. Spot-heat the bead then, using the tweezers to hold the shard, gently touch it to the heated spot to attach it to the bead. Using a brass shaper, gently heat and press it into place around the bead. For swirls, use a blunt glass stringer and spot-heat an area of the bead where you would like the swirl to be. Remove the bead from the flame and place the stringer into the heated spot and twist, hold for a second or two and then snap off the stringer, which will leave a raised swirl on the surface of the bead. Re-heat the whole bead to prevent cracking and repeat the swirls as required. The swirls can be left raised, melted smooth or 'capped' with a raised dot. Use the silver glass to place small raised dots around the bead. Use a reduction flame (i.e. turn up the propane or reduce the oxygen slightly) to bring out the golden lustre.

5 Place the bead in a kiln to anneal, along with two golden-lustre glass spacer beads to complete the piece. The beads should be cleaned before threading onto the paperknife. To fit the bead onto the paperknife, undo the stopper at the top, slide your bead and spacers on and re-screw the stopper to hold the bead in place.

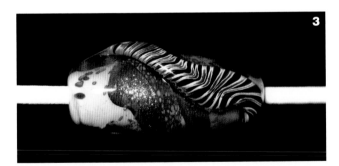

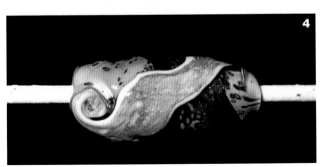

Butterfly Pate Knife

Try your hand at relief sculpture with this fairly easy decoration for the handle of a pate knife, created on a bicone bead, by Sabine Little. Make the flower and butterfly using stringers for crafting fine details. The bead is placed over the shank of the knife, so use a mandrel large enough to ensure that the bead sleeve is wide and long enough to cover the shank.

Materials and tools

For the bicone bead:

Large mandrel and thick bead release

Rod of white Effetre glass

Tweezers

Small pot of double helix gaia shards

Marbled rod in Vetrofond purplicious and white Effetre glass

1/16in (2mm) CiM creamsicle stringer

Rod of clear Effetre glass

Small pot of gold ruby striking frit

Karen Leonardo petal pullers (small)

Rake

Marver

1/16in (2mm) dark brown Effetre stringer

Hair-fine dark brown Effetre stringer

To complete:

Pate knife

1 Using the white rod, make a bicone bead, suitable in size to fit the width and length of the knife shank you will want to cover.

2 Using tweezers, attach the gaia shards to the bead. Melt these in completely or leave slightly raised, depending on your preference.

3 Use the marbled rod of purple and white to make five dots in a circle for the petals of the flower in the middle of the bead.

4 Rake each dot twice, once outwards and once towards the centre. Poke the middle and use the creamsicle stringer to place a central dot to create the middle of the flower.

5 Heat a small gather of clear glass and roll in the gold ruby frit. When it has melted in, pull a petal for the butterfly wing and attach it to the bead. Warm it through and gently marver it in, leaving it raised.

6 Repeat with the second part of the wing, pulling a slightly smaller petal. Attach it in the same way as above. Keep the whole bead warm as you work, especially the ends.

7 Spot-heat sections of the wings and rake them outwards. Rake the upper wing of the butterfly four times, and the lower wings three times. Keep the ends of the bead warm all the time.

8 Turn down the flame, and use the brown stringer to draw the body of the butterfly. Gently marver it into the bead, leaving it slightly raised.

9 Using the hair-fine brown stringer, add the antennae for the butterfly. Turn the flame back up and warm the whole bead through once more. Use a reduction flame (i.e. turn up the propane or reduce the oxygen slightly)

to bring out the shimmer in the shards and on the butterfly's wings. Put the bead in a kiln to anneal. Finally, slide the finished cover over the knife shank to attach.

Technique Tip

Handwash this knife in a mild detergent and dry carefully. Do not use a dishwasher.

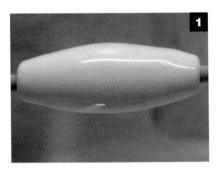

Ruffle Bead Spoon

Sabine Little shows you how to create a ruffle bead for a spoon handle. Created in dark blue with a series of four glass 'wheels' to create the ruffles, the gold leaf gives this bead extra glamour. Measure the depth of spoon mandrel and use this to determine the length of the bead, which will be threaded onto the spoon handle. If you are making a set of spoons, vary the colour for a personalized look.

Technique Tip

Handwash this spoon in a mild detergent and dry carefully. Do not place it in a dishwasher.

Materials and tools

For the base bead:

Large mandrel and bead release

Rod of dark transparent blue Effetre glass

Marver

Sheet of 24 ct. gold foil

Tweezers (or similar)

To complete:

Spoon, suitable for bead

1 Make a slim blue cylinder bead the width of the gap on your spoon handle. Marver into shape and check the ends as they will be difficult to adjust later.

2 At the end on the very left, create a small wheel by making one or two winds around the tube bead. Keep the wheel warm so it doesn't crack, but don't let it collapse.

3 Use the end of the mandrel to pull the rod to a thinner end for easier access to the other wheels, which you will be creating next. Do this whenever you feel necessary.

4 Use your thinned rod to build your second wheel. You are aiming for four in total, so space yourself accordingly.

This second wheel should be slightly larger than the first one, as one of the two central wheels.

5 Continue building two more wheels; another larger one and another small one at the very end. Make sure you keep the whole bead warm to avoid cracks. If you are left-handed, you might prefer working right to left.

6 Heat the bead evenly to ensure the wheels are properly attached. Try to avoid the wheels collapsing – if they do, use some flat tweezers to gently get them back into shape.

7 Heat the first wheel and use your tweezers to gently ruffle the edge. Continue to do so with all other wheels.

Be careful as you do this – this bead looks best when the wheels are not touching each other.

8 Heat the ruffled edges to ensure that the gold leaf will stick, then gently lay the leaf on top. Taking the leaf to the bead (rather than rolling the bead on the leaf) helps the ruffles to stay in place.

9 Gently use the tweezers to marver the foil into the ruffles. Tweezers – or another small tool – allow you to get round the ruffles and into crevices where an ordinary marver can't reach. Give it a final warm-through and put in the kiln. Later, attach this bead to the spoon. Unscrew the silver ball at the top of the spoon. Thread the bead on and reattach the silver ball.

Floral Beaded Pen

Sabine Little describes how to create two easy flower techniques by making five round beads in two colours. Each bead is decorated with stringers to make petals for flowers, poking and raking the dots. The beads are used to decorate a pen.

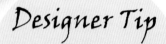

Materials and tools

For the beads:

Rods and stringers in CiM elphaba unique glass (green)

Bead-press (or marble press)

Rods in white Effetre glass (including prepared stringers)

Razor blade

1/16in (2mm) CiM pumpkin (light orange) stringer

Thick mandrels and bead release

Rake or pick

To complete:

Pen for attaching beads

Designer Tip

Pens on which to thread beads are available as lampwork accessories. Use spacers to fine tune the spacing of the beads if necessary.

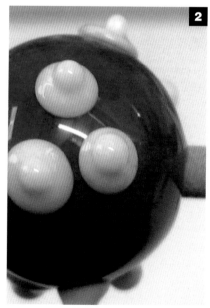

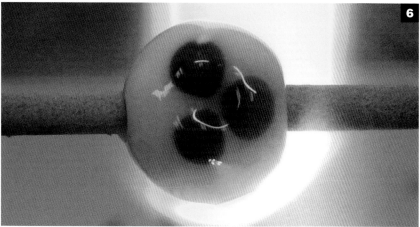

If necessary, move the razor blade slightly towards the middle of the dot as you press down, to correct the shape.

4 With the pumpkin stringer, place a small dot in the middle of each flower. Melt in gently before warming the whole bead through. Repeat to make three green beads and put in a kiln for annealing.

5 For the white beads, make a white bead in the smallest bead press cavity, then place three groups of three green dots around the bead, as above. Spot-heat the centre of each group of dots, and poke with a rake or pick.

6 Keep the bead moving in the flame to evenly melt out the poked hole. As the bead evens out, the dots will appear raked towards each other. If necessary, return the bead to the press to shape it. Warm gently through and place in kiln for annealing. Repeat the process in order to make two more white beads. When the beads are complete, thread the beads onto the pen and secure.

1 For the first green bead, make a round bead and shape it. Use a bead-press (or marble press) to help create the shape – you don't really need to use the top of the press; just use the bottom of the press as you would a marver.

2 Using the prepared white stringer, place three dots fairly closely together in a triangular shape. Repeat twice more around the beads, so you have three groups of three.

3 Preheat each dot before using a razor blade to mark it in half with the crease pointing towards the centre.

Urn Bead

Dawn Lombard shows you how to transform a cone-shape bead into an urn bead. This is a particularly useful skill for making necklaces. You can use the handles separately and attach a chain, silk, or ribbon to each side. Another design variation is to simply put a silver chain through one of the handles, which allows the bead to freely dangle from the chain.

Materials and tools

For the bead:

Prepared mandrels and bead release

Rods in a choice of colours

Large paddle marver

Frit

Silver leaf

Tungsten pick or round brass reamer

For the necklace:

Decorated lampwork bead

Cord

Silver wire for fixing

Clasp

1 Create a small donut bead in a colour of your choice. Use the marver to flatten the bead to create a small cylinder bead. Add more glass to correct the ends of the cylinder if they are not even.

2 Continue to build the cylinder length by following the step above. With each additional 'bead', ensure that the cylinder keeps a good shape. It is very important to make sure your ends are evenly shaped. If they are not, add more glass and use the marver to square them up.

Technique Tip

Heat control is one of the most important aspect of this project. If there is too much heat when making the handles, the handles will collapse.

3 Once you have achieved the desired length of bead, start to build up layers of glass on an angle. Put more layers of glass on one end and then taper the layers as you move down the length of the bead. At this point, the bead will have lumps and bumps.

4 Put the glass back in the flame and heat to a slightly molten stage. Hold the marver. Put the bead back in the flame to get it molten and marver again. It takes about ten repetitions to achieve a smooth cone shape.

5 There are a number of techniques that can be used to achieve a perfectly flat-bottomed cone bead. One way is to heat the large end of the bead and roll the mandrel against the edge of the marver. Another technique is to heat and tap the bead against the edge of the marver.

6 Now you can decorate your bead. Frit is placed on the bead, melted in and marvered smooth. Then a piece of silver leaf is applied and marvered smooth as well.

7 Create another bead slightly above the wide end of the cone. Use the edge of the marver and roll the bead into a short cylinder – as you do this it will fuse to the cone (base) bead. If the cylinder does not have the depth or length you require, simply add more glass and marver flat.

8 Keep the base bead warm and place a dot of glass at the top and bottom of the neck – where the handle will be. Continue to apply dots on alternative sides, each more angled towards each other, until they touch. Follow this same technique on the other side.

9 Work the bead further outside of the flame and warm the handle. This will smooth out the dots. As you do this, don't forget to keep the base bead warm. Use the rounding tool (pick or reamer) to smooth the handles to your desired shape. Anneal your bead in the kiln. Make a simple necklace, by adding a lampwork bead with silver wire to attach to a cord. Add a neck clasp of your choice.

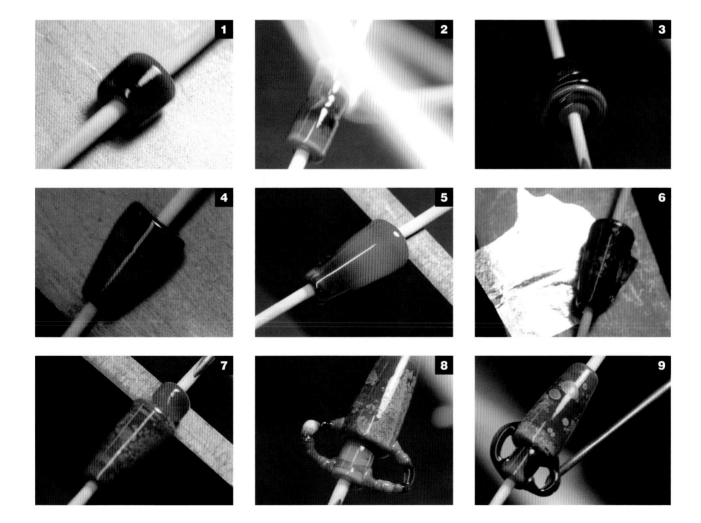

Cone Pendant

The pendant by Dawn Lombard begins with a single bead, rolled flat to create a cylinder. The shape of the bead is built up with glass and is 'angle marvered' to achieve a cone shape and then decorated. The bead can then be wired simply to make a classic, elegant pendant necklace.

Materials and tools

For the bead:

Prepared mandrel and bead release

Rods in a choice of colours

Large paddle marver

Silver leaf

For the necklace:

Silver fixings

Stainless steel cable

Coloured stringers

Clasp

1 Create a small donut bead in the colour of your choice. Use the marver to flatten and create a small cylinder bead. Correct the ends if they are not even by adding more glass.

2 Continue to build the cylinder length by adding additional length to the cylinder bead. With each additional

Designer Tip

Simple components are the best for decorating a large focal bead. The bead stands out as a piece of 'art' without getting lost.

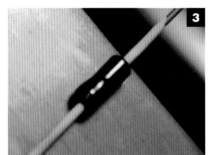

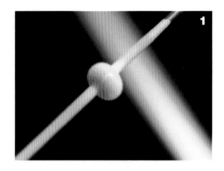

'bead', ensure your cylinder keeps a good shape. Flatten the additional length with the marver.

3 It is very important to make sure your ends are evenly shaped. If they are not, add more glass and use the marver to square them up.

4 Once you have achieved the desired length of bead, start to build up the layers of glass on an angle. Place more of these layers on one end and then taper the layers as you move down the length of the bead. At this point, the bead will have lumps and bumps.

5 Put the glass back in the flame and heat to a slightly molten stage, before using the marver to shape it.

6 Hold the mandrel at a degree angle and roll against the marver. Put the bead back in the flame to get it molten and marver again. It takes about ten repetitions of this step to achieve a smooth cone shape.

7 There are a number of techniques that can be used to achieve a perfectly flat-bottomed cone bead. One way is to heat the large end of the bead and roll the mandrel against the edge of the marver. Another is to heat and tap the bead against the edge of the marver.

8 Now you can decorate your bead. Put a piece of silver leaf on the marver, heat the bead, and roll it over the silver to attach it. Next, apply random dots of colour and melt them in.

9 After each layer of decoration, roll the bead on the marver on an angle to smooth out the bead. When you are happy with your shape and decoration, anneal the bead in the kiln. Make a simple necklace, perhaps attaching it to a classic stainless steel cable and using a Sterling silver tension clasp to hold and fasten the bead at the back.

Technique Tip

Create a perfectly shaped bead before starting your decorative work. It is difficult to correct the base shape if you have already started your design work.

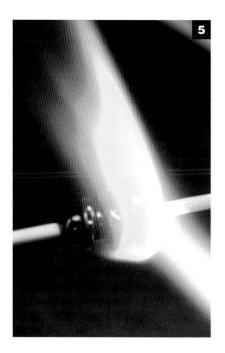

Beads for Rings

You may have seen those 'add-a-bead' bracelets and necklaces. Now you can wear replaceable large-hole beads on your fingers. These funky rings allow you to easily change your bead so you can match your entire wardrobe. Dawn Lombard shows you how to make the perfect shape and size bead to fit this cool new ring with one simple tool.

Materials and tools

For the beads:

5mm prepared mandrels and bead release

Rods in a choice of colours

'Donut' CGBeadroller

Frit, stringers, raku, foils or leafs in your choice of colour

Clear glass

For the rings:

2 x ¼in (6mm) Sterling silver grommets

Tweezers

Quick-bonding glue (Loctite premium liquid super glue)

⅜in (8mm) interchangeable bead ring

Large-hold spacer beads (optional)

1 Create a basic bead footprint in the colour of your choice. Ensure your wrap of glass has crisp edges (that are symmetrical) or the bead will be wobbly when worn. Once the initial wrap is placed, add a second full wrap of glass to the bead. The glass will slump down as you melt it and this will produce a nice pucker effect on each end.

2 Test the fit of your bead in the beadroller (roll the bead in the cavity) to determine the appropriate size. The bead should not completely fill the cavity of the form as you will be adding more glass. (Any of the top three sizes are perfect for the ring.) However, you may need to add extra glass to ensure a proper fit.

3 Decorate the bead using stringers, frit, raku, foils or leafs. You can also add a clear encasement during this step. Do not add too much glass to your base bead or you will increase the overall diameter of the bead – making it too large for your ring.

Technique Tips

The footprint of your bead needs to be symmetrical or you will end up with a lopsided bead.

It takes practice to master the CGBeadroller, but once learned, it is indispensable.

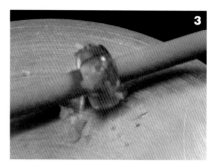

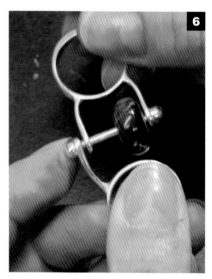

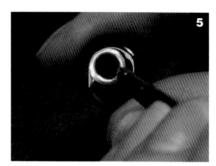

4 Use the beadroller once again to ensure a properly formed bead. Twirl your marver in the cavity of the form so that the glass takes on the shape of the mould. Once you have the desired shape, flame polish (in furthest part of the flame) the bead to remove any chill marks from using the marver.

5 Anneal the bead in the kiln. It should then be cleaned using a diamond reamer. Place a small ring of quick bonding glue on the rim of the bead. Pick up one of the silver grommets with tweezers and place onto the bead.

Ensure that the cap is secure by pushing down on the top of the cap with the tweezers. Proceed with placing the second grommet and let it dry for ten minutes.

6 Once the bead is completely dry, open the interchangeable ring and slide the bead onto the bar. If there is too much movement, large-hole spacer beads can be added to the bead ring to fill in the extra area. Keep in mind that you can also make smaller beads and wear two beads at once. Be creative with it and have fun.

Designer Tip

Rings are a great way to show your personal style. Match your bead ring with similar colours or go for a high-contrast colour.

Swirl Bead Pendant

With a clever use of gravity and spectacular Triton glass, Amanda Muddimer shows you how to create beautiful beads that are ideal for turning into simple, but striking pendants.

Materials and tools

For the bead:

Prepared mandrel and bead release

Rod in white Effetre glass

Hand-pulled stringer from Double Helix Triton glass

Marver

Rod in CiM blackcurrant glass

For the necklace:

Headpin

Wire wrap

Silver bail

1 Wind a base bead onto your mandrel to make a cylinder by adding wraps of glass using the white rod. Make the bead any length you wish for your own pendant.

2 Gently marver the cylinder bead into shape. You will be adding coloured ends to the bead so this will add to its final length.

Designer Tip

Triton is a good reducing glass to try. You can create a range of colours including silver, pinks, greens and blues.

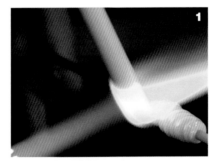

Technique Tip

When the glass is in the flame keep rotating the mandrel in one direction only to create the effect by gravity.

3 Add stripes of the triton glass stringer down the length of the bead. These will make swirling effects. You don't have to be too particular about the ends of the stringer as you should be aiming for effect rather than precision.

4 Go back to the flame and, using the heat close to the torch nozzle, heat up one end of the bead. Turn the mandrel in one direction only. When the glass is moving, lift up above the heat, keep rotating and let gravity do its work. Repeat on the other end of the bead. Reshape using the marver once the required effect has been achieved.

5 Add blackcurrant glass to both ends of your cylinder bead. Ensure the bead remains warm throughout the shaping process. It is very easy to forget one end while concentrating on the other!

6 Marver the bead into a cylinder shape once again as it may have become distorted.

7 Make a reduction flame (i.e. turn up the level of propane or reduce the oxygen slightly). Waft the bead into the yellow flame. The triton glass will show its effects very quickly.

8 Once you are happy with the effect and you have finished marvering, put the bead into a kiln for annealing.

9 Using findings of your choice, simply place the bead into a headpin and wire wrap the top onto a silver bail to attach to a necklace.

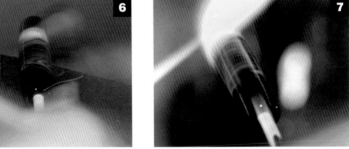

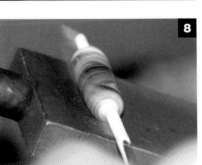

Victoriana Bead

Amanda Muddimer shows you the process of making a bead by mixing colours and silver glass to create lovely effects. As a follow on, the hole through the bead is lined with silver at its core.

Materials and tools

Prepared mandrel ¼in (6mm) and strong bead release

Rod of CiM adamantium glass

Rods of white Effetre glass (also used for prepared stringers)

Rod of CiM leaky pen glass

Rods of Davinci 2 silver glass (also used for prepared stringers)

3D flower rod tool

Rod of CiM clear glass

Rod of amethyst Effetre glass

Super tungsten poker or sharp tool

Tweezers

Designer Tip

Experiment by mixing colours of silver glass and pull stringers for wonderful effects.

1 Wind a base bead in adamantium glass onto your mandrel. Apply blobs of white glass using the rod around the four quarters of the bead. Use a white stringer to apply smaller dots in the gaps towards the mandrel. Melt the dots in slowly. Apply leaky pen glass blobs over the top of all the white dots and repeat the two layers, melting the glass in slowly between each application.

2 Using the silver glass rod for the quarter dots and a stringer for smaller dots, apply blobs over the layered dots on the bead and again melt in gently until the bead is round.

3 Heat each of the quarter large dots in turn and use the 3D flower rod to push the centre of each dot inwards, creating a dimple. Repeat for the three other quarter dots around the bead.

4 Using a rod of clear glass, heat a large blob of glass and apply it over the dimple on each quarter dot. This effect will give extra depth to the dot, helping the flower to 'float' above the previous layers. Slowly melt in the glass as you round up the bead.

5 Using the silver glass stringer, apply four small dots in the shape of a flower to each quarter dot. Melt in and apply clear amethyst dots followed again by silver dots melting in each layer slowly as you go.

6 Heat each quarter dot in turn. Remove the bead from the heat and poke the centre of each flower using a sharp tool to do this, such as a super tungsten poker.

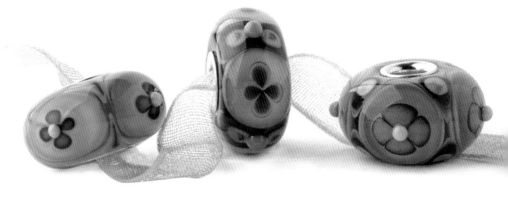

7 Keep the bead warm, being careful not to melt in the hole that you have just made. Whilst doing this, melt a large blob of clear glass on the end of your rod. Apply the clear glass to the quarter dots in turn, keeping each application warm as you go. When four quarters are covered with clear glass, apply heat to each of the quarter dots in turn.

8 Flatten using a handheld marver, making sure the flower and layered blob are covered as much as possible.

9 Gently and slowly heat your bead melting in the clear and rounding up your bead as you go. You need to be patient, heating the bead slowly and gently for the best effects. Put your bead into a kiln to anneal.

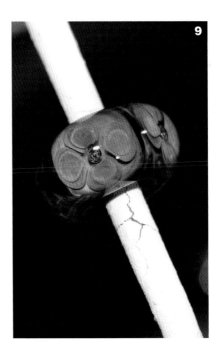

Victoriana Silver Core

The silver coring of beads has come a long way in recent years; there are now bead presses that can be used to line lampwork beads which makes the process much simpler and ensures fewer breakages. Amanda Muddimer shows you how to drill out and clean your bead before lining it with suitably sized silver tubing and using a special bead press. The silver should move with a little freedom within the hole of the bead.

Materials and tools

Victorian bead (from previous page)

For silver core:

¼in (6mm) Sterling silver tubing (thin walled)

Permanent marker

Pipe cutter

Stanley knife (or de-burring tool)

Cook's blowtorch (or jeweller's torch)

Pickle

Jim Moore bead press (or similar press)

Dremel (or similar rotary tool)

1 Measure the length of the silver tubing leaving approximately ⅛in (3mm) each side of the hole. Using a permanent marker, mark the place you will need to cut.

2 Using a pipe cutter, cut the tube where you have marked it.

3 To remove unwanted edges, de-burr the ends you have cut using either a Stanley knife or a special de-burring tool. You should end up with neatly cut ends with no sharp edges.

4 Anneal the silver to a soft rose colour using a small cook's blowtorch. Hold it for a few seconds and quickly quench in cold water. Then put the silver into pickle (an acidic solution) to remove the fire stain.

5 You can now use one of the many presses available to gently flare the edges of the silver. Turn the bead over between presses to ensure each side is the same. Do it slowly and watch the silver as it gently flares and fits itself to the contours of your bead.

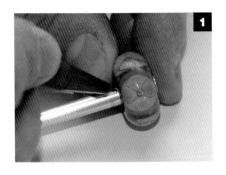

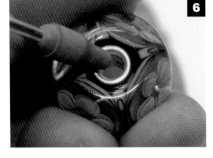

6 Polish your bead using a rotary handheld tool, with polishing burrs in different grades finishing up with an extra fine and a good rub on a polishing cloth.

Technique Tip

The size of the silver tube can be a little tricky as bead release on your mandrel can vary in thickness. However, a ¼in (6mm) tube is a comfortable fit if using a ¼in (6mm) mandrel.

Peacock Bead Bracelet

The ornate focal bead by Lorna Prime has a beautiful gold-lustre finish with the odd flash of silver. Delicate feathers in turquoise are scattered over the surface. Vintaj findings in the bracelet help to frame the focal bead. Dragonflies hover between Czech glass faceted turquoise Picasso donuts and the bronze chain, and a brass leaf toggle clasp finishes it off.

Materials and tools

For the bead:

Prepared mandrel and bead release

Thick white Effetre rod and stringer (prepared)

Thick dark transparent turquoise Effetre stringer (prepared)

Thick transparent light violet Effetre stringer (prepared)

Silver foil

For the bracelet:

20in (50cm) 20g vintaj bronze wire

6½in (17cm) antique bronze mother son chain

5/32in (4mm) brass round spacer

3 x 5/32in x ¼in (4mm x 6mm) pale blue Picasso faceted rondelle

2 x 5/8in (18mm) antique bronze filigree flexible bead caps

2 x brass dragonfly connectors

4 x 5/32in x ¼in (4mm x 6mm) turquoise Picasso faceted rondelle

Brass leaf toggle clasp

1 Add white glass onto a mandrel and make a lentil-shaped bead. Burnish silver foil over the entire surface.

2 Using the white stringer, lay a double trail of eight dots along the length of the bead with a single dot at the finish. Repeat on the opposite side. Repeat in between these two trails but with four dots and a single dot to finish.

3 Take the turquoise stringer and add a dot over each of the white dots. Melt all the dots in flat.

4 Take the transparent violet stringer and place a dot in the centre of all the turquoise dots. Melt all the dots in flat.

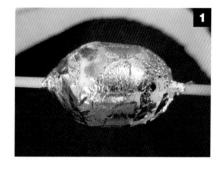

5 Spot-heat one of the trail of dots. Place the turquoise stringer at the base of the top single dot and very gently, but quickly, drag the stringer through the centre of the trail of dots to feather them. Now gently tack the stringer onto the surface. Repeat the dragging with the other trails of dots. Reheat the bead and press and fire polish off any chill marks. Place in a kiln to anneal.

6 Cut a 1in (25mm) length of bronze wire and wire wrap the loop end of the toggle onto it. Add the small brass spacer and wire wrap another loop and trim off the excess wire.

7 Cut a 4in (100mm) length of bronze wire and wrap it onto the previous loop. Add a pale blue rondelle, brass flower bead cap, focal bead, bead cap and a pale blue rondelle and bead cap. Half-wrap another loop and attach the ¾in (20mm) and 2¾in (70mm) length of chain. Complete the loop to secure the beads and trim off. Bend the petals on the bead caps so they fit snug.

8 Wrap another 1in (25mm) piece of bronze wire onto the last link of the short piece of chain. Add a turquoise rondelle, half-wrap a loop and attach one of the dragonflies to complete the loop. Wire-wrap another link with a turquoise rondelle onto the tail of the dragonfly and attach the 2¼in (55mm) length of chain. Using these techniques attach a dragonfly onto the 2¾in (70mm) length of chain. Now two linked chains come from your bead.

9 Cut a 1in (25mm) length of bronze wire and half-wrap a loop. Attach this to the last link of the long chain and the bottom loop of the last turquoise faceted link. Add a pale blue rondelle. Half-wrap a loop and attach the other half of the clasp. Complete and trim off the excess wire.

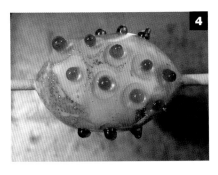

Celestial Bead Bookmark

This decorative bookmark by Lorna Prime was designed around the celestial pattern on the bookmark hook. Calming deep blue makes up the focal bead, while the surface at one end is ivory glass. Finishing touches include bicone crystals and tiny twinkling silver star charms that are wire-wrapped onto a dangle that has a leopardskin jasper round.

Materials and tools

For the bead:

¼in (6mm) thick silvered ivory stringer (prepared)

Prepared mandrels and bead release

Rod of silver glass (Double Helix Kronos)

Rod of pale blue Effetre

Sphere press (or marver)

Dentist's pick or raking tool

For the bookmark:

4in (10cm) length of 20-gauge silver wire

3-link length of chain

7 x headpins

2 x ⁵⁄₃₂in (4mm) daisy spacers

⅜in (8mm) leopardskin jasper round

3 x small star charms

7 x ⁵⁄₃₂in (4mm) bicone crystals (Montana Swarovski)

Bookmark hook

4 x ¼in (6mm) jumprings

1 Prepare by making a thick silvered ivory stringer (see page 69). Now make a cylinder bead using the silver glass. Place the cylinder into a reduction flame (i.e. increase the propane or reduce the oxygen slightly) to bring out the metallic sheen of the silver glass.

2 Using the pale blue glass, encase the cylinder sufficiently to make a round bead. Use a sphere press as a marver to help this process along. Using the silvered ivory stringer, make a few wraps on one end of the bead by the hole to cover about a third of the bead. Melt the silvered ivory stringer and re-shape your bead.

3 Spot-heat the surface of your bead where the silvered ivory joins the blue. Take the pick and just touch it on the surface of the bead. Rake the glass towards the opposite bead hole, away from the silvered ivory. Repeat twice more at intervals around the bead.

4 Repeat the previous step, but this time raking towards the silvered ivory bead hole in the gaps between the previous rakings. Re-shape the bead and place in a kiln to anneal.

5 Take the piece of silver wire and wrap the length of link chain onto one end.

6 Take a headpin and thread a daisy spacer and the leopardskin jasper round onto it. Wire-wrap this onto the bottom link of the chain.

7 Attach one star charm per link on the chain using the jumprings.

8 Thread one bicone crystal onto each of the remaining headpins and wire-wrap two onto each link of the chain. Place them either side of the link.

9 Take the last daisy spacer and thread onto the silver wire, followed by your bead and the last bicone crystal. Wire-wrap a loop to secure all beads onto the wire and attach a jumpring. To finish, simply add the completed charm to a bookmark hook.

Sea Anemone Pendant

The pendant is made out of clear borosilicate glass with a coloured pattern inside the glass. Marcel Rensmaag helps you master the art of trapping air bubbles in a glass disk to create a sea anemone pendant. This style of pendant has a simple shape, but looks very intricate with its design.

Materials and tools

¼in (6mm), ⅜in (10mm) and ½in (12mm) clear borosilicate glass

Northstar dark blue amber/purple stringer

Pin frog

⁵⁄₃₂in (4mm) clear borosilicate stringer

Peter's tweezers (or similar)

⅛in (3mm) tungsten pick

Paddle marver

Pointed-nose tweezers

Technique Tip

Allow plenty of preparation time for this project. Take it slowly.

1

1 Prepare a gather of glass by melting a $\frac{25}{64}$in (10mm) handle approximately 4in (10cm) to a $\frac{15}{32}$in (12mm) rod that is 2½in (6cm) long. This size of the handle is easiest to rotate when making this pendant. Heat the point of the rod to form a gather at the end.

2 Press the gather end onto a marver into a disk (a 'maria'). Heat the face of the maria to make it soft, so when pressed onto the pin frog it will create dents in the glass. Once you have dents on the face of the disk, the disk needs to be covered with glass to make air bubbles.

3. You can use several different types of glass to do this. A stringer made out of dark blue amber/purple is used to make the dots.

4 Apply the dots of glass to the disk over each dent or indentation. When the dots have been applied, melt them flat with the glass using a neutral flame.

5 You are now ready to get the dots into the glass to form the anemone. You should continue to heat the edges of the disc to ensure the outside will concave and the surface of the disc looks a bit like a bowl.

6 Gently press the disc on the marver. Remember to let gravity do most of the work. If you press too hard your pattern will become distorted. Repeat this step until you are satisfied and the pattern is deep enough in the glass. If you have done it correctly you will see the pattern shrink on the surface of the disc.

7 The pattern will now be sunk deep into the glass gather. Now is the time to stop the process, by gently removing glass from the back of the anemone using a stringer. This can be tricky so take your time.

Designer Tip

Use different colours to give the pattern more of a 'flower' effect or a background on the pendant to create more contrast.

8 If the process is successfully carried out you will have all the lines coming into a star-shape pattern.

9 Heat the back of the piece and press it into a marble mould to make it rounded. Now put a $^{15}/_{64}$in (6mm) punty with a cold seal on the back of the pendant.

10 Focus the heat on the front of the pendant and remove the glass blank with the handle that is left. Gently melt the glass to form the lens. Take your time, because the lens must be perfect for the effect of the sea anemone.

11 Remove the punty from the back by first putting the remaining punty on the bottom of the pendant with a cold seal and tapping of another one on the back.

12 Put a small gather on the topside of the pendant and melt to form a dome -like shape. Dent the sides with Peter's tweezers to make the hole. Repeat this action and gently wiggle the tweezers up and down to break through the glass. You can use a tungsten pick to widen the hole of the loop. Now heat the pendant and warm the pointed tweezers. Grasp the loop with the tweezers and remove the bottom punty. Flame polish away the punty marks and place the glass in a kiln to anneal.

Graceful Eastern Bead

This versatile bead, crafted by Anita Schwegler-Juen can be used for making bespoke jewellery pieces or for decorating mandrel accessories such as pens or letter openers. For this project, the bead has been completed as a pendant decorated by small glass beads, fresh-water pearls and silver charms.

Materials and tools

For the bead:

Rod in white Effetre glass

Prepared ⅛in (3mm) mandrel and bead release

Rods in transparent violet and new violet Effetre glass

Steel rake

Rod in CiM lapis (blue)

Rods in coral, yellow and periwinkle (light blue) Effetre glass

Rod in CiM lipstick (brick red)

Paddle marver

For the pendant:

Jewellery pliers

Silver wire

Silver ring

Glass beads, fresh-water pearls, silver charms

Bead caps

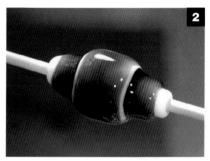
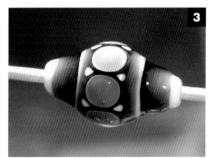

1 Make the cylinder bead in white. The cylinder should be about 1¼in–1½in (3–4cm) long and about ½in (10mm) thick in diameter. Make sure the ends are parallel and even. Encase with a thin layer of violet to about ⅛in (3mm) on both edges of the cylinder.

2 Apply a thin layer of white. This layer is applied from the centre to about ¼in (6mm) to the edge of violet. Encase the white part completely with violet.

3 Add dots of lapis onto the middle of the violet, at regular intervals. With a white stringer, place small fine dots either side of the large lapis dots. Melt all dots regularly and carefully. Add white dots on to the lapis dots, then cover with violet and melt all carefully.

4 Now hold the mandrel vertically into the flame and heat the centre of the bead by turning the mandrel in a constant flow until the glass begins to flow. Repeat the whole process from the other side. Some pulled ellipses may develop from the previously applied centre dots.

5 Add small fine dots of new violet into the gaps of the ellipses. Add white dots onto these dots and violet dots on top of white dots. Melt these three layers of dots carefully.

6 Make sure that the bead is not too soft, then nudge the tip of a steel rake into the three-layered dot and drag the glass in the direction of the mandrel with just a little pressure on the surface.

Add small yellow dots to the raked outer dots and melt them carefully. Add the white dots and melt them, then cover with violet and melt them, too.

7 Add dots of lipstick to the centre of each ellipse and melt. Add another small dot of periwinkle and a small dot of white. Cover those two layers with violet and melt everything carefully. On top of the centre dots add white and violet dots. They should be connected to each other but still sticking out.

8 Finally, add ultra-small fine dots of coral. Carefully warm up the whole bead without melting any more dots and place in a kiln for annealing. To make the pendant: at one end of a piece of silver make an eyelet using pliers. Hook a silver ring into this loop. Add small glass beads, pearls and silver charms. Thread onto the silver wire a bead cap, the Eastern bead and another bead cap, then form another loop. Make sure no rough ends remain on the silver.

Funky Fish Earrings

This fish bead by Sue Webb is a fairly straightforward sculptured bead based around a twistie that can be made to create any design you like including flowers, dots or stripes. This sort of bead can also be used on its own to create phone charms, keyrings or pendants, or incorporated into jewellery for a touch of fish frivolity.

Materials and tools

For the beads:

Prepared mandrels and bead release

Rods of transparent yellow, mid-turquoise, light sky blue Effetre glass

Pale transparent rod for base bead

Marver

V-shaped tweezers (home fashioned)

Mini-mashers

Tungsten poke

Fine tweezers

Sharp-edge tool (chisel-shaped tool)

White, black and orange stringers

For the earrings:

2 x silver headpins with 3 loops

Blue crystal

Blue seed pearls

Findings

1 Make the twistie by heating ¾in (2cm) of two or three contrasting rods and attaching them flat against each other. Heat them evenly, including both ends. Once glowing, take out of the flame and twist and pull at an angle. The faster and harder you pull, the thinner the twistie.

2 Make the base bead and roll into a cylinder shape. Attach the end of the twistie to the left side of the cylinder, keeping the twistie to the edge of the flame. 'Walk' the bead up the twistie as it becomes soft. Do not rush this or the twistie will break off. Melt it in.

3 Flatten the bead on a marver on both sides. Reheat one side of the bead until it glows. Using a pair of V-shaped tweezers (or similar), squeeze one side of the bead into a point; this will be the head of your fish. Flash the bead in the flame to smooth out any chill marks.

4 Heat the other end of the bead until it glows, being careful not to lose the pointed shape you have just made.

Using mini-mashers flatten the outer corner and then the other corner. There should be a ridge left down the middle.

5 Warm one of these flattened corners but not so much that it loses its shape. Use a tungsten poke to nudge and flip up a ripple effect. If space allows on this side do the same in a downward direction. Now repeat this on the opposite side.

6 Carefully heat the middle ridge that is left and pull out the tip of it with tweezers to form the tail. Use a gentle flame so you don't melt away the ripples. If you want you can pull the tail round to one side to give a feeling of movement.

7 Use a white stringer on the topside of the head to make two raised dots and add little black dots on top. Melt them in so they are properly attached but leave them raised – these eyes are designed to be 'goggly'. Add an orange dot on the ridge of the nose and make a groove in the middle with a sharp edge; this should form some luscious lips!

8 Try and make two fish that match, at least in size. Now team up your fish with freshwater pearls, shells, little charms or something with a seaside theme. This fish has a headpin with three loops at the bottom. Above the fish is a little blue crystal.

9 To finish off, add some little blue seed pearls hanging from the bottom. Make a loop at the top and shorten and wrap the wire around for a secure finish. Attach the silver loop to a pair of silver findings.

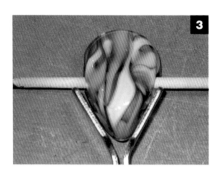

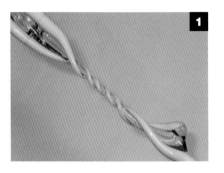
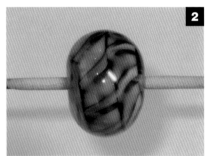

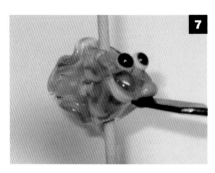

Twisted Light Pull

Sandra Young shows how to make a long, light pull with laid-on line decoration, using clear borosilicate glass. The light pull tapers up to a loop at the top with a shorter taper down to a point at the bottom. The tapers have a raised line twist going out to each point with the lines curling around each other on the bulb. Colour is added using ready-made lustres hand-painted and fired onto the surface of the light pull.

Materials and tools

4½in (12cm) length of ⅝in (16mm) clear borosilicate glass

4 x 12in (300mm) lengths of ⅝⁄₃₂in (4mm) clear borosilicate glass

Long-handled tweezers

Ready-made liquid glass lustres

Technique Tips

It is important to keep the glass at as even a temperature as possible throughout your working.

Always keep the glass moving in case the glass gets unevenly hot around the rod and the bulb becomes uneven or out of line.

1 Make a 4in (10cm) spill using 4in (10cm) of the ⅝in (16mm) glass and melting on ½in (10mm) handles at either end. Make sure the handles are in line with one another. If not, heat where the handles meet the spill, gently turn keeping the handles straight.

2 At 1¼in (30mm) from the end of the spill heat and build up your bulb, turning the rod steadily and keeping the same area of the rod continuously in the flame, without moving from side to side. Push together gently when the glass is soft enough, thickening the rod and creating a round bulb.

3 When the bulb is approximately ¾in (20mm), take it out of the flame, still turning until cool. Pick up a piece of ⁵⁄₃₂in (4mm) rod. Hold the spill at approximately 45° to the flame and underneath it. Hold the ⁵⁄₃₂in (4mm) rod at 90° from the spill, which should be about 45° from the flame on the other side.

4 Let a smaller hot flame catch the top of the spill and the end of a ⁵⁄₃₂in (4mm) rod. Draw it along the spill, maintaining the angles of the rod to the spill and flame. Draw around into a curl when you come onto the bulb and melt off the ⁵⁄₃₂in (4mm) leaving an upside-down question mark. Repeat around the spill four times. Anneal in a kiln.

5 Repeat the second step, starting from the middle of the curls on the bulb and curling in the opposite direction and then straight down to the bottom of the spill. Repeat from the middle of each of the other curls. Anneal, moving the spill from side to side through the flame as you continue turning.

6 Heat below the bulb and when the glass is soft, gently pull and twist, tapering evenly down but leaving the handle attached with ⅜in (8mm) of glass. Anneal the bulb and then heat above the bulb. Pull and twist steadily, taper to a point and melt the handle off.

7 Heat 1in (25mm) at the end of the taper until it begins to flow. Remove from the flame and, using the tweezers, bend the end over to form a loop. Carefully melt the end into the taper to close the loop. Gently heat the loop and make sure it is straight in line with your light pull. Anneal the whole light pull thoroughly.

8 Melt the handle back on to the top of the loop, keeping it as straight as possible in line with the light pull. Now holding this handle, heat the bottom taper gently and twist and pull the handle off. Anneal well and leave to cool. Carefully melt the other handle off, reshaping the loop with the tweezers, if necessary.

9 Hand-paint the light pull when it has cooled completely. Paint along the raised lines of the curls or inside them, or perhaps both in different colours, as you wish. Place in the kiln to anneal.

Ivy Leaf Pendant

This pendant was created by Sandra Young using clear borosilicate glass. The pendant has line detailing, with a loop for suspending from a chain, or cord, from the 'stem'. Colour is added using ready-made lustre that is hand-painted and fired onto the surface of the pendant.

Materials and tools

Length of 1/2in (10mm) clear borosilicate glass rod and a few lengths of 15/64in (6 mm) clear borosilicate glass rod

Paddle marver

A knife or sharp-edged tool

Long-handled tweezers

Ready-made liquid glass lustres

To complete:

Necklace of your choice

1 Melt a length of 15/64in (6mm) rod onto the length of 1/2in (10mm) rod to create a handle. When the rods are melted together, remove from the flame turning continuously, holding in a straight line until it has cooled enough not to move. The straighter the handle to the rod, the easier it is to work, enabling you to heat evenly around the rod to form an even bulb.

2 At the end of the 1/2in (10mm) rod, where it meets the handle, heat and build up a bulb of glass, turning the rod steadily and moving up the length of the rod slightly, pushing together gently when the glass is soft enough, thickening the rod and creating a rounded bulb approximately 3/4in (20mm) in diameter.

Technique Tip

Keep the glass at as even a temperature as possible: bear in mind the thin leaf glass loses its heat faster than thick glass.

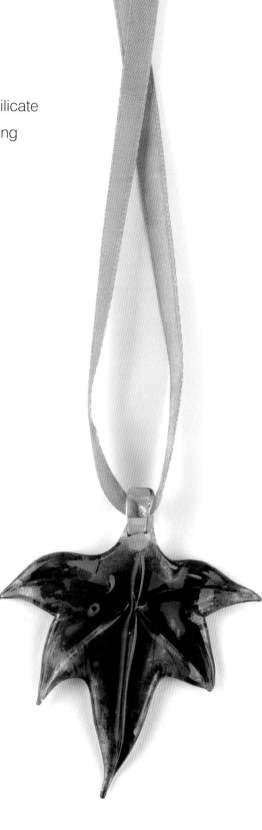

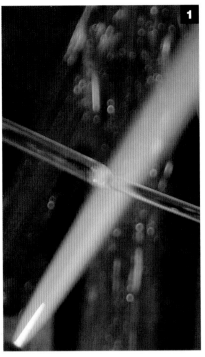

3 When the bulb is approximately ¾in (20mm), take it out of the flame, and place it on the marver. Before the bulb cools flatten it with the handled marver. You may need to reheat and flatten the bulb more than once. Make sure the whole of the bulb is heated evenly each time to produce a flat, round disk.

4 Move the flattened disk through the flame, keeping it predominantly edge on to the flame and moving from edge to edge to heat both to the same degree. When warm enough to move, gently pull to a point, forming a long flattened drop shape and melt off the ¹⁵⁄₆₄in (6mm) handle.

Technique Tips

When heating the flattened glass to stretch to a point, concentrate the flame a little more on the edges of the leaf. Move the flame back and forth along the edges prior to pulling gently.

Flame anneal at regular intervals as you work. If cracking begins to appear immediately flame anneal to try and recover your piece.

Working as quickly as possible will help you achieve a good result.

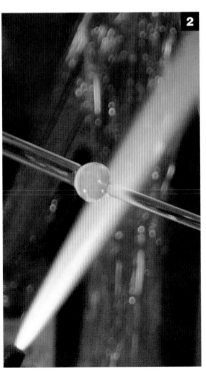

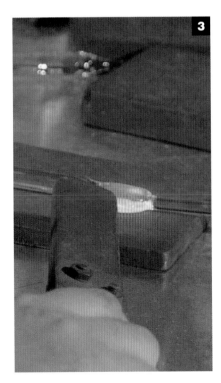

5 Now take a piece of ¹⁵/₆₄in (6mm) rod and holding the flattened drop at an angle to catch the edge of the flat near the handle, attach a small gather of glass from the rod to form a lobe. Repeat this process until you have two balls of glass on both edges of the flattened drop.

6 Heat all of the leaf and the balls of glass and place on the carbon flat and use the handled carbon flat to flatten them all to the same thickness as the main part of the leaf. You may need to heat and flatten these areas more than once. They will form the 'lobes' of the leaf.

7 Heat the leaf and, when it is hot enough to begin to soften, place it on the flat surface. Taking a knife make a line along the length of the leaf. You may need to heat the leaf several times to make a clear line along it. You have to mark the leaf quite quickly whilst it is still hot and, therefore, soft enough to mark.

8 Repeat this process, making a line along the middle of a lobe of the leaf to the central line along the middle of the leaf, to form a 'vein' to resemble a real leaf. Heat and make a line on each lobe; with each line meeting at the same point on the central 'vein' of the leaf.

9 Gently heat each lobe and, using tweezers, pull each one to a point. You can curve the lobes down towards the main point of the leaf by pulling gently round towards it. Work carefully and make sure you do not get the tweezers in the flame.

10 Melt on a ¹⁵/₆₄in (6mm) handle to the main point of the leaf, keeping the rod and handle in as straight a line as possible, turning continuously out of the flame until cool enough not to move. This will make the next step easier. Ensure the join is thick enough not to snap when you swap hands to make this the handle for the next step.

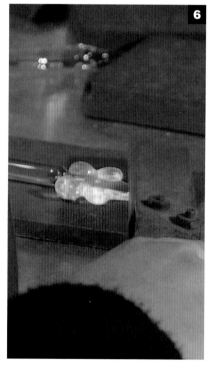

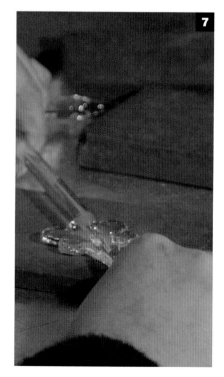

11 Swapping the $^{15}/_{64}$in (6mm) handle to your right hand, heat and pull the $^{1}/_{2}$in (10mm) rod handle from the join of the leaf, leaving a length of about 1in (25mm), $^{1}/_{8}$in (3mm) thick glass. Gently heat this length and, using a pair of tweezers, bend over at right angles to the flat of the leaf, to form a loop. Melt to the leaf top.

12 Holding with tweezers, melt off the $^{15}/_{64}$in (6mm) handle. Hand-paint the leaf with glass lustre when it has cooled completely. Place in the kiln to thoroughly anneal and colour the leaf pendant. Allow the kiln to cool and then remove the pendant from the kiln and attach to the necklace.

Glossary

Anneal Heating a piece of glass until its temperature reaches a stress-relief point. At this point the glass is still too hard to deform, but is soft enough for internal stresses to ease. The piece is then allowed to heat-soak until its temperature is uniform throughout.

Aventurine (Also known as goldstone) This is a type of glass contains a lot of metal oxide (usually copper), giving it a metallic sparkle.

Bead release A mixture of alumina and high-fire clay, making up a thick clay-like solution. This is applied to a mandrel to allow for the release of the glass bead once the glass has cooled.

Borosilicate glass Hard glass used in laboratory equipment and for cookware, glass blowing and glass sculpture as it has a low CoE. This makes this glass resistant to temperature changes, making it easy to work without thermal shock and breakage.

Brass press Used to mould glass into uniform shapes. This tool comprises of two parts: the base of the press sits flat on the workbench, while the adjoining upper part of the press fits neatly over the lower section. When the molten glass is placed into the mould, it is shaped when the press is engaged.

Cane Pulled rods of glass which are used for decorative purposes. They can be plain, contain patterns or be twisted.

Chromatic implosion A special bead where the shape is determined by continuing to let the wheel run down the mandrel into a tube or 'bone' shape – this type of bead is an excellent way to work on your control of gravity, since you are only letting the glass flow alongside the mandrel.

Coefficient of thermal expansion (CoE) The rate at which glass expands when heated. Glasses with differing CoEs are not compatible because of the changes taking place on the molecular level, they will crack or break apart when cooled.

Dichroic glass (Dichro) This glass has a protective coating of clear glass. It contains layers of tiny vaporized particles of metal, which give off various shades of colour and light reflection.

Didymium glass A special glass that absorbs the bright yellow sodium flare to allow safe working in a flame. Didymium is used in freestanding protective glass frames, face shields, clip-on glasses and in a variety of spectacle frames. It offers some protection when using MAPP gas or propane torches with soft, soda-lime glass.

Enamels Very fine particles of ground glass. Enamels are a very versatile material to use with glass as they broaden the colour palette and give countless different effects for beads.

Fibre blanket Used to cool a lampwork bead slowly if a kiln is not available to anneal the finished beads. It is a white fire-resistant heat insulation material, used for fire-resistance and heat preservation.

Fire polish Bathing a lampwork bead in a neutral flame once it is finished gives it a glossy shine without losing its shape.

Beads can also be strengthened by flame polishing where glass flows filling any cracks or surface scratches.

Filigrana glass Murano glass, made up of colourless rods, in which coloured or opaque white threads are enclosed. The term filigrana also covers all styles of decoration in which threads of glass are embedded in clear glass to form a very fine network pattern.

Flash-heat To flash-heat a bead in the flame is to give it an intense flash of heat to the outer layer of glass.

Foil leaf (Foil or metal) A thin foil used for decoration. Metal leaf can come in many different shades. Gold, silver, copper palladium and aluminium leaf are all used for decorative purposes.

Footprint The initial wrap or laying down of molten glass on a mandrel that is used to form a bead. This footprint often determines the finished size of the bead.

Frit Small chunks or fine chips of broken glass. Frit can be reduced in size using a crusher. It is normally used for the surface decoration of glass.

Gather The term applied to the glass melted on the end of a rod, often just before laying the footprint on a mandrel or pulling a stringer.

Lustre A sheen or reflective surface, such as when special paints are applied to glass.

Mandrel A stainless steel rod used for winding on glass. Mandrels come in various sizes.

Marbled rod A mixture of two or more rods melted together in the flame and mixed in a random manner to produce a mottled effect. The gather is pulled into a useable rod or stringer.

Mica powder Purified and crushed mica minerals. It is available in a variety of different colours from dazzling silver or gold to muted tones. Some mica powders have a shimmer effect, so they are also called 'glitter'.

Marver Flat pieces of graphite or other metal used for shaping glass. To marver is the act of shaping glass.

Mashers Long-handled metal tools used to flatten or shape glass.

Millefiori A mosaic glass cane made up of decorative images, so the various colours join to form patterns in the pulled glass. When cooled the cane is cut into slices.

Murrini A glass cane made by layering up hot bits of coloured glass, so the various colours join together to create pictures in the pulled glass. When cooled the cane is cut into thin chips.

Oxy-con A machine that makes oxygen, as used by lampworkers. For lampwork torches that need a mix of gas and oxygen it is a cost-effective and safe way of producing the oxygen part of the mix.

Parallel mashers Tools designed for quick and efficient flattened beads. Some mashers are adjustable with a screw mechanism that will control how flat the mashers press the glass bead.

Peter tweezers A pair of tweezers with ends that are bent over at right angles so that they touch each other. Used when creating loops to hang pendants.

Puckers Little dimples at the holes of beads. It is desirable for them to be slightly indented into the hole, round and smooth.

Punty A metal, iron or glass rod on which molten glass is handled when being shaped and worked. It is attached to the glass and used to hold, rotate and spin the work in progress.

Raku A type of glass normally used as frit that produces a wide range of vivid colours when superheated.

Reamer Usually a small metal round file or tool used for cleaning out the bead release that remains in the hole of a lampwork bead once fired and cooled. Bead reamers can also be battery-operated tools, with replacement tips.

Reduction glass Glass colours that react to a reducing flame, often with metallic or devitrification effects. The flame that is used to bring out the colours in glass contains less than normal levels of oxygen and an abundance of fuel.

Scum Tiny bubbles that appear when glass is heated, particularly if the glass is scratched or has imperfections. Scum can be burned off when heated at a higher temperature.

Silvered glass Specialist glass that has a metallic content that reacts when bathed in a reduction flame to produce a mixture of vibrant colours and effects.

Silver ivory stringer A dark ivory rod covered in silver leaf, heated and pulled into a stringer for decorative use.

Sodium flare The bright yellow ball of light seen when the naked eye views the flame of a lit torch. While sodium flare is not hazardous, it is difficult to see through. Filtering it out using a pair of Didymium glasses allows the lampworker to see their work and the glass as it changes temperature.

Striking glass The process of cooling and reheating glass through one or more cycles in order to develop its colour. Some glass will loose or change its colour when heated. This type of glass is referred to as striking glass. If the colour of the glass completely disappears, striking is then necessary to regain colour.

Stringer A thin, straight and long piece of glass used to add additional glass to areas in order to fill in places or to even up edges, or to add decorative patterns.

Twistie Pulled glass that is twisted as it is being pulled into long thin rods.

Vermiculite A hydrated basaltic mineral. It is used to help slowly cooled lampwork beads to avoid stresses, before they are annealed.

Zirconia Cubic zirconia (or CZ) is the cubic crystalline form of zirconium dioxide. The synthesized material is hard and usually colourless, but may be produced in a variety of different colours. Zirconia is frequently used in lampwork beads as it can tolerate high temperatures.

Contributors

ABOUT THE AUTHOR

JOAN GORDON

Joan Gordon is the former editor of UK's leading craft magazine: 'Making Jewellery', a GMC Publication. She is a freelance author, jewellery maker, teacher and designer. Joan has been involved in the craft industry for approximately thirty years. She lives several months of the year in Queensland, Australia. As an international consultant Jean travels extensively; the UK is considered her home away from home. Nature provides her with much of her design inspiration. Working with precious metals and lampwork are Joan's favourite crafts. Having worked in an industry alongside a diverse and varied group of artisans, she never tires of experiencing first-hand, new and innovative techniques. Joan enjoys experimenting with glass and combining lampwork beads with alternative mediums. She is constantly looking for new ways to use glass in decorative and practical projects. Her aim in writing this book has been to provide a practical resource for those interested in exploring lampwork as a craft, to showcase the talents of professional lampwork artists and to share inspirational methods for using lampwork beads to make jewellery and items for the home.

ABOUT THE TECHNICAL ADVISOR

LESLEY RANDS

Initially inspired in childhood by the 'glass man' she saw year after year at the local fair, Lesley began experimenting with various forms of glass art. She successfully created a range of Bristol Cobalt Blue Glass jewellery suitable for both men and women. With the support of her husband David and her wonderful children Lesley now devotes her time to beadmaking and the challenge of mastering the many skills involved in creating miniature works of art. Lesley has contributed to both the Melting Glass and Decorative Techniques sections of this book, as well as assisting in several of the other chapters.

www.lesleyrands.com

ABOUT THE ARTISTS

ELAINE ALHADEFF
Grecian Vessel Pendant

Elaine studied lampwork and jewellery design and fabrication at the Pratt Fine Arts Center in Seattle. Since 1993 Elaine has been working with hot glass, precious metals and fine gemstones, as well as sharing her knowledge with classes and workshops. Elaine lives in Washington, USA. A lot of her inspiration comes from her Mediterranean heritage. Elaine's work has been exhibited internationally.

www.MeandYouArtwear.com

www.mayabeads.etsy.com

EMMA BAIRD
Bead Earrings, Bead Ring

Emma is a Senior Art Clay Instructor based in Edinburgh, UK. She runs a wide variety of Precious Metal Clay courses, from those for beginners to the world-recognized Level I & II Certification Program. She is currently the Chairman of the Art Clay Guild in the UK and runs Art Clay Scotland in Edinburgh. Emma frequently designs mixed-media jewellery and loves combining her two passions – beads and silver. See more of Emma's work by visiting the website at Art Clay Scotland.

www.artclayscotland.com

BEVERLEY HICKLIN
Encased Bead Bracelet, Champagne Bead Stopper

Beverley is a lampwork artist based in the UK whose background in textiles (originally graduating from Winchester School of Art with a degree in textile design) and love of colour and movement is reflected in her work. She offers lampworking classes at her studio near Horsham, West Sussex.

www.beverleyhicklin.com

PAULINE HOLT
Squiggle Bead Necklace, Catwalk Necklace

'Jazzy Lily' (Pauline) lives and makes jewellery from her home studio in beautiful Buckinghamshire. She first joined a glass beadmaking course in 1997. The challenge of heating glass and shaping it into a miniature work of art that can be worn is something that she still finds magical. Pauline co-founded Glass Beadmakers UK in 1999. In 2001 she began teaching lampwork and now teaches regularly at her own studio.

www.jazzylily.com

JAN JENNINGS
Grapevine Pendant, Organic Paperknife

Jan was originally inspired to make beads after a trip to Murano in Venice, Italy where she watched local beadmakers at work. Today, she creates lampwork beads from her small home studio set within the beautiful North Yorkshire Moors National Park. It is from these surroundings and a love of nature that she gains much of the inspiration for her work, which is usually in the form of colourful floral beads or textured organics – and often with a hint of sparkle!

www.crystalgarden.co.uk

SABINE LITTLE
Butterfly Pate Knife, Ruffle Bead Spoon, Floral Beaded Pen, (Chromatic Implosion)

Sabine is a lampwork artist and jewellery designer living in the beautiful Peak District. She has been silversmithing since 2005, and took up lampworking to complement her designs. Sabine teaches lampwork techniques for beginners and sculptural beadmaking to more advanced students from her beautiful two-torch studio. She also regularly contributes to magazines in the UK and Germany.

www.littlecastledesigns.co.uk

DAWN LOMBARD
Urn Bead, Cone Pendant, Beads for Rings

Dawn experienced a profoundly soothing connection with glass at an introductory lampwork bead class. She set up a studio with a friend to continue this passion. To refine her skills, she has attended classes by leading artisans. She is fascinated by the combination of creativity and scientific complexity of working with glass. Dawn creates earthy and organic style beads in her two studios (Monroe and Watertown, Connecticut, USA) and is the founder of Lavender Dawn.

www.LavenderDawnJewelry.blogspot.com

AMANDA MUDDIMER
Swirl Bead Pendant, Victoriana Bead, Victoriana Silver Core

Amanda is a full-time lampwork bead artist specializing in silver core beads and pendants. She was one of the first lampwork artists in the UK to develop her own process in creating silver core beads, which has contributed to the success of her business. Amanda specializes in this area and has developed a range of pendants and other pieces of jewellery, which are both distinctive and easy to wear. Amanda teaches from her studio in north Devon.

www.mangobeads.co.uk

LORNA PRIME
Peacock Bead Bracelet, Celestial Bead Bookmark

Lorna started to design jewellery and beaded accessories as a hobby in 2003, first teaching herself lampworking with a Hot Head torch in her coal shed. Lorna is inspired by Asian mandala patterns. Primarily designing with lampwork beads, Lorna likes to use gemstones and only the finest quality findings to produce her one-of-a-kind pieces. Lorna also offers tuition in lampwork glass beadmaking (with a dual-fuel torch) from her home studio.

www.pixiewillowdesigns.com

MARCEL RENSMAAG
Sea Anemone Pendant

Marcel works from an art studio in the Netherlands, where he spends most of his time creating glass art. About six years ago he discovered lampwork and found it complemented his interest in glass art, so began his quest in lampworking. Marcel often draws inspiration from nature.

www.beadartists.org

ANITA SCHWEGLER-JUEN
Graceful Eastern Bead

'UNIKAL Glasperlendesign Atelier im Woeschhuus' is the label of a small glass-studio, also called Atelier (Workshop) in Woeschhuus, which was open by Anita and her husband near Zurich in Switzerland in 2006. In addition to the manual production of lovingly and carefully crafted glass beads, blown glass and glass sculptures, the glass studio offers workshops with both local and international artists. The project was written by Elias Schwegler-Juen and translated by Daniela Ellenberger.

www.das-unikal.ch

SUE WEBB
Funky Fish Earrings

Sue has always been involved in various craft activities. A former psychiatric nurse, today she works full time in Bristol as a lampwork artist and also teaches lampwork. Her jewellery is inspired by a variety of sources. Sometimes it can be by what she is wearing that day, her children's homework, a walk on the beach or a trip to the zoo. Most of her jewellery has a novelty signature bead such as a bug, snake or fish. Sue makes use of freshwater pearls, semiprecious stones, soapstone, shells and coral in her work.

www.suewebb.co.uk

SANDRA YOUNG
Twisted Light Pull, Ivy Leaf Pendant

Sandra has been lampworking since 1984. Having learned the basic techniques by making glass ships contained in bottles, she continued and developed her own individual style, gradually finding ways of working on progressively larger scales and refining the detailing skills, to create magical and mythical sculptures, as well as jewellery inspired by nature. Sandra undertakes varied commissions from her studio near Pewsey, Wiltshire, and wants to pass on her skills and experience to others.

www.firecreation.co.uk/glass

Resources

General contacts that you may find useful for lampworking and, in particular, undertaking the projects in this book. If you search online you will find many other similar suppliers.

UK

Beads Direct
21 Gordon Road, Meadow Lane
Industrial Estate, Loughborough,
Leicestershire LE11 1JP
Tel: +44 (0)1509 218 028
www.beadsdirect.co.uk

Creative Glass
2 Sextant Park, Medway City Estate,
Rochester, Kent ME2 4LU
Tel: +44 (0) 1634 735 416
www.creativeglassshop.co.uk

Diamond CZ
Coppethorn, Village Cross Road,
Loddiswell, Kingsbridge, Devon TQ7 4RQ
www.diamondcz.co.uk

Electric Kilns/Cherry Heaven
Tel: +44 (0) 1929 477 137
www.electrickilns.co.uk

Hamilton Taylor Ltd
Unit 1, Kinning Park Business Centre,
544 Scotland Street West, Glasgow,
City of Glasgow G41 1BZ
Tel: +44 (0)1414 290 102
www.off-mandrel.com

Hot Glass
Melanie Wilson, 72 High Street,
Syston, Leicester LE7 1GQ
Tel: +44 (0)116 260 4442
www.hot-glass.co.uk

Manor Optical Co.
Manor House, Dudley Road,
Halesowen, West Midlands B63 3LG
Tel: +44 (0)121 550 2609
www.manor-optical.co.uk

Plowden & Thompson
Dial Glass Works, Stewkins,
Stourbridge, West Midlands, DY9 4YN
Tel: +44 (0)1384 393 398
www.plowden-thompson.com

Rashbel UK
24–8 Hatton Wall, London EC1N 8JH
Tel: +44 (0)207 831 5646
www.rashbel.com

Schott Glass UK
Drummond Road, Astonfields
Industrial Estate, Stafford ST16 3EL
Tel: +44 (0)1785 223 166
www.schott.com/uk

Tuffnell Glass
Church House Farm, Main Street,
Rudston, East Yorkshire YO25 4XA
Tel: +44 (0)1262 420 171
www.tuffnellglass.com

Warm Glass UK
5 Havyat Park, Havyat Road,
Wrington, Somerset BS40 5PA
Tel: +44 (0)1934 863 344
www.warm-glass.co.uk

USA

Arrow Springs
Tel: + 1 (800) 899-0689
www.arrowsprings.com

A.R.T.C.O
Tel: +1 (408) 288-7978
www.artcoinc.com

Burgard Studio
Tel: +1 (505) 872-9486
www.burgardstudio.com

Cattwalk Lampwork Tools
Tel: +1 (973) 398-7390
www.cattwalk.com

Coe90.com
Tel: +1 (888) 213-8588
www.coe90.com

C&R Loo
1085 Essex Avenue, Richmond CA 94801
Tel: +1 (510) 232-0276
www.crloo.com

Double Helix Glassworks
2540 Crites Street SW Ste B,
Tumwater, WA 98512
Tel: +1 (360) 754-9555
www.doublehelixglassworks.com

Franz Art and Glass Supply
130 West Corporate Road,
Shelton WA 98584
Tel: +1 (360) 426-6712
www.frantzartglass.com

Generations Glass Lampworking Supplies
PO Box 747, 108 N Railroad Street,
Kenly, NC 27542
Tel: +1 (888) 456-7975
www.generationsglass.com

Glass Diversions
Tel: +1 (317) 797-9144
www.glassdiversions.com

Jim Moore Glass Tools
P.O. Box 1151, Port Townsend, WA 98368
Tel: +1 (360) 379-2936
www.toolsforglass.com

Northstar Glassworks
9386 Southwest Tigard Street, Tigard, ORE
Tel: +1 (503) 684 6986

Sundance Art Glass
6052 Foster Road, Paradise CA 95969-3121
Tel:+1 (800) 946-8452
www.sundanceglass.com

Australia

Bead Glass
Tel: +61 (02) 4379-1302
www.beadglass.com.au

Chockadoo Art Glass and Supplies
Tel: +61 (02) 9639-4529
www.chockadoo.com

Gem World
1908 Sandgate Road, Virginia, QLD 4014
Tel: +61 (07) 3865-4404
www.gemworld.com.au

Organizations and information

The Society for Glass Beadmakers:
www.gbuk.org

The International Society for Glass Beadmakers: www.isgb.org

British lampwork showcase:
http://britishlampwork.co.uk

Creative Glass Guild:
www.creativeglassguild.co.uk

Corina Tettinger: www.corinabeads.com

Effetre: www.effetre.com

Murano glass: www.murano-art-glass.com

GMC magazine website:
www.makingjewellery.com

Other Sources

A selection of websites related to glassworking at www.dmoz.org

Art in Architecture Press: Specializing in books about glass and glassworking techniques.

Coatings by Sandberg: Manufacture of dichroic glass.

Colored Sands Glass Co: Glass-blowing supplies, tools and torches.

Dichroic Alchemy: Custom dichroic glass images and dichroic/trichroic borocoatings.

Electroglass Furnaces: Electric glass, melting furnaces and annealers.

Frantz: Glass rods, tubes, tools and supplies for lampworking.

Generations Glass: US East Coast glassblowing and lampworking supplier.

Glass Notes: Guide for the building of and maintainance of a glass studio.

Glass Supply: Selection of tools, supplies for blowing, accessories and starter kits.

Gordon Glass Company: Tools and several accessories, such as diamond bits or cutters for working with glass and mirror.

Glassy House Supply: Borosilicate glass, millifiori and murrini. Distributes glassblowing supplies and lampworking tools.

Harmony Stained Glass: A wide selection of glass, tools, books, patterns and kits.

Heritage Glass: Glass beadmaking supplies, tips for making glass beads and classes (in Texas).

Hot Fusion Studio: Dichroic glass patterns for the hot-glass artist. Custom colours and designs available.

Hot Glass Color & Supply: Glass blowing supplies including Kugler-colors, dichroic glass, tools and heat protective gear.

Hub Consolidated, Inc: Glass blowing equipment and tools, including melting furnaces, puntys and torches.

Malacaster Bicknell Co. of New Jersey: Glass tubing, colour borosilicate rods, blanks, equipment, torches and supplies.

Olympic Color Rods: Glass colour rods and accessories for lampworking and glassblowing.

Ozziebuddy: Equipment, tools and supplies for the Australian and European market.

Photo Blanks: Specialize in handcrafted glass paperweights to showcase mementos and make gifts.

Rainbow Glass: Kilns from several different manufacturers.

Steinert Industries: Glassblowing tools including blowpipes, optic moulds and cane marvers.

Tracy's Stained Glass Workshop: Supplies for stained glass, warm glass, mosaics and beadmaking.

Two Lasses Glass Classes: Dichroic and patterned fusing glass, fusing supplies, tools, equipment and books.

Wale Apparatus: A variety of products for the novice up to the expert glassworker.

Acknowledgements

From the author

My thanks go to Lesley Rands for her hard work and dedicated hours at the torch. Thanks also to her husband David for his expert photography.

To all the artists who have contributed projects for the book, the editorial staff at GMC including Beth Wicks, Sarah Doughty, Gerrie Purcell, photographers Rebecca Mothersole and Anthony Bailey and designers Chris and Jane Lanaway. Thanks also to Martin Tuffnell at Tuffnell Glass, Benjamin Evers at BE Glassworks, Canada, Robin Cameron of Cherry Heaven and the online shop Electric Kilns.

Picture Credits

p2: Emma Baird; p3: Anita Schwegler-Juen; p8: Amanda Muddimer (top), Marcel Rensmaag (btm); p9: Jan Jennings (top) Elaine Alhadeff (btm); p10: iStockphoto; p11: iStockphoto, except Beth Wicks (middle top); p12–13: Emma Baird; p22: David & Lesley Rands (top and middle), Sandra Young/Sean Brown (btm); p24–5: Sabine Little; p26: David & Lesley Rands; p27: David & Lesley Rands, except Sabine Little (bottom left); p28: David & Lesley Rands; p29: David & Lesley Rands, except Tuffnell Glass (top); p30: Pauline Holt (top right); David & Lesley Rands (middle and btm right), Tuffnell Glass (top left); p31: David & Lesley Rands; p32–3 David & Lesley Rands, Carlisle Machine Works; p34: David & Lesley Rands; p35: David & Lesley Rands (top), Marcel Rensmaag (btm left), Sandra Young/Sean Brown (btm right); p36: David & Lesley Rands; p37: Paula Paton (top), Pauline Holt (middle right); p38–9: Robin Cameron – Electric Kilns; p40–41: David & Lesley Rands; Melting Glass and Decorative Techniques step pictures by David & Lesley Rands, with the exception of p102–103 by Sabine Little. Step pictures: p108–111: Elaine Alhadeff/Steven S. Policar of MarkFocus; p112–117: Emma Baird; p118–123: Beverley Hicklin; p124–7: BH Associates/Brian and Pauline Holt; p128–131: Jan Jennings; p132–7: Sabine Little; p138–141: Dawn Lombard/Patrick Manning; p144–9: Amanda Muddimer; p150–153: Lorna Prime; p156–7: Marcel Rensmaag; p158–9: Anita Schwegler-Juen; p160–161: Sue Webb; p162–7: Sandra Young/Sean Brown; p168–9: Emma Baird; p170–175 photos supplied by contributors; p180: Emma Baird. Final images of projects and beads photographed by Anthony Bailey. Cover and part opener photography by Rebecca Mothersole.

Index

b/11 - C
12/11 H
5/12 W
11/12 O

To place an order, or to request a catalogue, contact:
GMC Publications Ltd, Castle Place, 166 High Street, Lewes, East Sussex BN7 1XU
United Kingdom
Tel: +44 (0) 1273 488005 Fax: +44 (0) 1273 402866
www.gmcbooks.com